Effective Teachi

A practical guide to improving
your teaching skills

Philip Allan Updates
Market Place
Deddington
Oxfordshire
OX15 0SE

Orders

Bookpoint Ltd, 130 Milton Park, Abingdon, Oxfordshire, OX14 4SB
tel: 01235 827720
fax: 01235 400454
e-mail: uk.orders@bookpoint.co.uk
Lines are open 9.00 a.m.–5.00 p.m., Monday to Saturday, with a 24-hour message answering service. You can also order through the Philip Allan Updates website: www.philipallan.co.uk

ISBN 978-1-84489-526-7

© Philip Allan Updates 2007
Design and illustrations by Neil Fozzard
Printed by Hobbs the Printers Ltd, Hampshire

Environmental information
Philip Allan Updates' policy is to use papers that are natural, renewable and recyclable products and made from wood grown in sustainable forests. The logging and manufacturing processes are expected to conform to the environmental regulations of the country of origin.

Effective Teaching

A practical guide to improving your teaching skills

Contents

Introduction

Teaching, like many jobs, can be demanding, stressful and tiring, but at the same time it is an important, worthwhile and stimulating profession that involves a wide range of skills, strategies and techniques. As an effective and successful teacher you will not only have the ability to raise standards but will have all the skills necessary to provide pupils with the kinds of positive learning experiences that will help them to become successful adults.

This guide assumes that teaching skills can be learned and developed. If you are a teacher who is just starting your career you may have fewer skills, techniques and strategies to fall back on. You should find that there are many sections here that will help you to become more effective. If you have been teaching for many years it is still possible to benefit from new ideas and develop and improve all the successful techniques that you use every day in your classroom. In fact, the best teachers, whether experienced or newly qualified, are always learning and reflecting both on what they can do successfully and what they might need to do to improve.

Successful teaching is not just about natural gifts that you either do or do not have. Some teachers are naturally gifted, but this may be because they never stop learning how to do their jobs more successfully. So while natural gifts may be true of a small minority, assuming that this is all there is to teaching can be damaging to many teachers who are experiencing crises of confidence, and who are starting to lay the blame on their own inadequacies rather than the lack of particular skills that can be practised and learned.

It would be futile to try to cover every aspect of what effective teaching actually is. But it is important to remember that as a teacher you do not teach in isolation. You are part of a whole school or a whole department or faculty. How this larger group is managed and how the school or department is led is important in terms of ethos and culture, as well as how professionals work alongside each other and how you and your pupils relate to one another. At the same time, you will need to know as much as possible about pupil behaviour, classroom control and classroom management. Behaviour management is an emotive subject and one that receives a lot of attention from the public in an often sensational way. It is always part of the teaching agenda and this book includes suggestions on how to improve and manage poor behaviour.

Inevitably there is some 'content' overlap. For example, behaviour management does not exist in isolation. Teachers who plan thoroughly and are able to differentiate work for different levels of ability usually have the kinds of classroom management skills that mean there are fewer opportunities for poor behaviour.

This means that those teaching skills required for general classroom management are closely linked to those required for managing behaviour. It is also true that similar techniques, for example, are needed to raise pupils' self-esteem and to break down the barriers presented by reluctant learners. Rather than refer backwards and forwards to strategies and techniques that are similar or common to various different chapters, on most occasions they are repeated. This means chapters can be read separately in their own right.

One of my main arguments, especially in the first two chapters, is that when you are teaching you should never feel that you are on your own, and that any problems you have should, where possible, be shared with colleagues. If this happens at a productive level (and it usually does) everyone should benefit. With this in mind, I have suggested that there should be whole-school or whole-department policies as well as a whole-school or whole-department ethos. You may feel secure with the idea of a whole-school approach or, if you work in a very large school, be more involved at department or faculty level.

You do not need to read this guide in chapter order. While there is a pattern to the ideas that are developed, one chapter does not necessarily have to follow another in terms of content and understanding. All the chapters have some activities. They have been written to extend the text and to offer opportunities to try out some of the ideas at a practical level. These can be completed individually or by groups as part of professional development. They do complement the text and while it is not essential to use them all it is important to look at them. I have tried throughout the guide to suggest some key skills that will make you a better and more confident teacher. With this in mind, lists and checklists are included, which you can measure yourselves against.

Finally, it is important to emphasise that, although there are all kinds of effective teaching techniques and ways of organising and managing classrooms, there is no single correct 'technology' of teaching. Ultimately, all of us have to be sufficiently flexible throughout our careers to adapt methods and styles to circumstances that are generated by the interaction between pupils, curriculum content and the teaching and learning processes.

Roger Smith

1 The individual, the department and the whole-school team

This chapter emphasises the importance of working in an effective and well-organised team, and suggests that you are more likely to be successful and find your job stimulating if you are part of a professional group of colleagues who are able to influence and support you. The whole school/department can have a significant effect on each teacher. However, we must recognise how important it is for the individual to know what is to be achieved and how to do it. Each of us has to approach each group of pupils assertively and with a sense of confidence in who *I* am and what *I* want to do.

In fact, we all need to ask ourselves several key questions:
- What do *I* actually do as a teacher?
- What will the pupils actually do in *my* lessons?
- What will the pupils *I* teach learn?
- What use is this learning to the pupils *I* teach and the school *I* work in?

What kind of teacher am I or do I want to be?

All of us have been at school and have been pupils. You will have been exposed to the skills and eccentricities of numerous teachers. We should all be able to remember something about this experience. **Activity 1.1** (p. 26) requires you to make a list of positive and negative views about teachers who taught you. It is well worth thinking about this and transferring your thoughts about 'good' and 'bad' teachers — what they did and how they influenced you — to your own teaching.

Some of the positive attributes of 'good' teaching should include the following:
- delivering the curriculum effectively using a variety of techniques
- using praise and encouragement appropriately
- not using sarcastic put-downs or ridicule
- having realistic sanctions and using them
- saying no — meaning it and taking action every time it is necessary
- promoting a calm, purposeful learning atmosphere
- not building up petty incidents out of proportion, but at the same time not allowing low-level disruption of any kind
- believing in a strong work ethic

- setting realistic targets, goals and deadlines
- having high expectations
- insisting on positive on-task behaviour
- having a belief that learning should be as interesting as possible
- differentiating the work so that it is appropriate for all pupils
- observing classroom work and constantly feeding back to pupils their successes and how they need to improve

How do I relate to my colleagues?

You are an important individual, and how effective and successful you are and how you work, behave and react with your colleagues and with pupils will have a bearing on how effective your whole department, faculty and school will be. There is further discussion on working with colleagues in Chapter 7, but at this stage we need to examine how you think about yourself and how you relate to other teachers and colleagues.

Most of us know how we feel when we are working. We can have emotions such as being 'happy', 'trusting', 'powerful', 'stressed' etc. and at the same time we can also feel that we would really like to be seen differently by our colleagues. For example, imagine you are looking dishevelled, rushing from room to room with armfuls of paperwork and are obviously stressed and appear to have no time to relax. Do you really want colleagues to see you this way? Ideally, wouldn't we all like to be seen as calm, well groomed, up to date with all our paperwork and having all the time in the world because we are professionally on top of our jobs? The self-recognition chart in **Activity 1.2** (p. 27) provides a useful way of looking at yourself in relation to colleagues. If we are good at picking up clues from colleagues about our own abilities and how we work alongside them, it will make us much more effective and our professional relationships much more successful. Finding out what our colleagues feel about us is not easy and it is made even more difficult because they will all have a range of different ideas, abilities, backgrounds, personalities, knowledge and experience. It is hardly surprising that working together as an individual within this kind of group or team is fraught with problems. But you have to be able to work with other people. Even the most brilliant teacher — and I will stress this over and over again — cannot work in isolation and will sometimes have to work in a group or team for many different reasons. Changing from group to group, and by implication working with different colleagues, can trigger a range of emotions as well as a range of professional — and less professional — responses. These can include feeling more secure, using matching strengths and balancing weaknesses to create a more effective working partnership, uniting through some common purpose or, in an autocratic environment or at a time of rapid change, forming a group for self-protection.

Being reflective in terms of relationships with colleagues, while demanding a certain amount of perception, can also be just about knowing who likes who, who can work better together, who dislikes who and who respects you professionally. One way of understanding how this works is by completing the staff relationship grid in **Activity 1.3** (p. 29). The grid was developed at seminars held at the Open University Summer Schools for the Reading and Language Diploma and used in Easen (1985).

Of course, ideally, we would all like to be able to place our colleagues at the high end of each axis, so that they all respect our professional performance and at the same time like us. Unfortunately, professional life is not that simple. What is important is that if we do have colleagues who don't like us or don't like what we are doing professionally then we need to think about what we should do. On the other hand, we may actually have the misfortune to work with people who are themselves not very likeable and not particularly effective professionally. Here, too, you need to consider what to do. Whatever the case, teachers teach and pupils learn and we have to be able to work together professionally within an ethos or atmosphere that helps this to happen and standards to rise.

School or department 'atmosphere'

Each one of us will bring our own styles, skills and techniques to our work, but how we use these strategies will be partly determined by how effective the whole team is in the process of teaching and learning, and how easy or difficult it is to work with our colleagues. In many ways, teachers need to fit the schools they are working in. This is why effective teaching needs to be looked at in its context and why each of us needs to consider ourselves against the background of where we work, who our colleagues are, what they do, how they work and what they are like.

Very often the most effective schools or departments are the ones that are exciting and enthusiastic places. They won't have just happened by accident, but will have been organised and planned by successful leaders who have been allowed to develop their skills at all kinds of levels, from classroom teachers upwards. It is this effective leadership that drives the school forward and produces a positive atmosphere, which is usually reflected in committed teaching and higher standards. It is important to establish the characteristics of an effective school or department because it is this foundation that helps determine how good the teaching is and how positive and enthusiastic individual teachers are. In other words, all the classroom strategies and teaching styles operated by teachers and all large-scale whole-school/department projects will at worst fail or at best operate at a much less efficient level unless there is, as the Elton Report (1989) suggests, 'a positive whole-school atmosphere'. This will include:

- **Shared values** — there needs to be an agreed way of doing things and a consensus on 'how we do things around here' that each teacher follows.
- **Strong leadership** — as well as the obvious patterns of leadership through head teachers and deputies, most heads of department, subject leaders and teachers are leaders. They all need to be strong and assertive and all need to embody the same core values.
- **Strong beliefs about teaching and learning** — there should be agreement about what constitutes good practice and good teaching. All teachers should follow the agreed good practice and be supported and helped by their colleagues.
- **Joint planning and problem-solving taking place through meetings** — core beliefs and the positive ethos of the school are constantly reinforced through efficient teams.
- **Balancing change** — there is an appropriate balance between new ideas, innovation, tradition and any need to change.
- **Participation in decision-making** — teams are recognised as the main focus of effectively maintaining the positive whole-school culture.

Whole-school ethos

The ethos or culture of each school or department is usually an amalgamation of social, moral and academic values. It can influence and determine how pupils and teachers relate to each other as well as defining relationships in terms of courtesy, care and consideration, helpfulness, cooperation and respect for others. The right ethos will mean that classroom management, what is taught, how it is taught and what needs to be taught is agreed by everyone, owned by them and is, because of this, more successful. Conversely, an inappropriate or badly thought-out ethos will mean that even teaching that is well prepared and well structured will be more difficult to implement.

Indicators of a positive ethos within a school do not have to be complex and can include simple ideas such as:
- Pupils are happy.
- Pupils work hard.
- Pupils are treated fairly.
- Bullying is a rare occurrence.
- Everyone receives help socially and academically when they need it.
- There is a lively, creative atmosphere.
- Teachers motivate pupils.
- Discipline is positive and consistent.
- All those working in the school or visiting it are made to feel welcome.

While schools cannot totally eliminate the effects of social deprivation, academic ability, attitudes to learning and differences between children, they can, through their own successful practice, raise standards. This is not a new concept. As early as 1979, Rutter et al. reached several conclusions about how whole schools can influence teaching and learning. It is worth reading the following two extracts. The italics are mine:

> It is not argued that schools are the most important influence on children's progress, and we agree...that education cannot compensate for the inequities of society. Nevertheless, *we do suggest that schools constitute one major area of influence and one which is susceptible to change*. (p. 182)

> How was it that 12 schools set up to undertake the same task with children from much the same geographical area came to develop such different styles? Doubtless part of the answer lies in the history of the schools and in a variety of external factors outside their control. *In addition, however, the schools' expressed philosophies and chosen ways of working were important*. (p. 203)

One important question that needs to be asked is how does the ethos and atmosphere of your school/department make a positive difference? The message to both teachers and their leaders/managers is that they have the power to create an ethos that improves both the standards of teaching and the standards of pupils' work and, subsequently, their life chances. Mortimore et al. (1988), writing about primary schools, suggested what is now accepted as a fairly standard list of what needs to happen in order to create a positive ethos. I see no reason why this should not apply equally to secondary education:

- There is strong, effective and powerful leadership at all levels.
- All teachers are involved in decision-making and feel that they 'own' those decisions that directly affect them.
- There needs to be whole-school/department continuity and consistency in terms of discipline strategies, homework policies, teaching methods, resource management, timetable structures etc.
- Structured, well-paced, lively teaching needs to be matched to pupils' needs.
- All teaching should be intellectually challenging for all pupils.
- The environment of the school will be task- and work-orientated and every pupil will recognise that learning is the norm rather than the exception.
- Adults and pupils will communicate a lot both inside and outside the classroom.
- Record-keeping and assessment will be sensible and thorough and will be communicated to parents when necessary in ways that they are able to understand.
- There will be a positive climate where emphasis is placed on praise rather than criticism.
- Control in classrooms is firm, fair and consistent with pupils being treated as individuals.
- Activities are organised to take place before and after school as a means of offering pupils wider experiences.

Many of these factors may seem obvious, but part of the success of each school or department will be built on whether a list of 'aims' such as those described above can be acted on by all teachers.

Every Child Matters

The green paper *Every Child Matters* was a consultation paper published in 2003 and it was followed, after a period of consultation, by *Every Child Matters: Change for Children* in December 2004. It sets out a national framework and agenda for local change with the main aim of providing more accessible services focused around the needs of children, young people and families. In other words, one of its main aims is to ensure that there is closer liaison with the NHS, police and social services. The reason why this is important to you — and why it is included here as part of a whole-school/department emphasis — is because the document identifies five excellent and worthwhile outcomes for all of us to take on board and which should be part of any whole-school/department ethos:

- **Be healthy** — enjoying good physical and mental health and living a healthy lifestyle is important, and every teacher and every school need to play a leading part in health education, including questioning the value of snacks and the nutritional content of school meals. There has been some progress in the fact that smoking by 11–15 year olds has decreased since 1996, but levels of obesity are rising. Although sex education is having some impact, with teenage conception rates lower than they were in 1998, they are still the highest in western Europe.
- **Stay safe** — pupils need to feel that they are being protected from harm and neglect. A study of offending and victimisation among 11–16 year olds in mainstream schools found that almost half (46%) had been the victim of some kind of bullying offence in the last year. We must continue to make behaviour management and anti-bullying an important issue.
- **Enjoy life and realise potential** — pupils need to get the most out of life and develop the necessary skills for adulthood. There are all kinds of statistical reports claiming that expected academic levels at most, if not all, ages have risen. These improvements must be balanced against continuing problems with boys' achievement, inconsistencies across different ethnic groups and an unauthorised absence rate that remains both consistent and unacceptable.
- **Contribute to the local community** — children and young people need to be involved in their local community and not engaging in anti-social or offending behaviour. Once again, how we teach citizenship, how we provide links to pupils' own communities and how we manage behaviour and attitudes is increasingly important.

- **Achieve a good standard of living** — pupils must not be prevented by economic disadvantage from achieving their full potential in life. We will have to develop strategies to enable all pupils to reach their full potential and to break the cycle of poverty. Children and young people from workless households or where parents are on low incomes must be encouraged to aspire to better careers and lifestyles.

Whether we like it or not, teachers are closely involved in *Every Child Matters* and our teaching may have to widen its scope because we are in a prime position to:
- influence the behaviour and attitudes of pupils
- continue to raise standards
- provide a central community focus
- begin to influence parental attitudes

Many of the concepts in *Every Child Matters* are not new; teachers have been keen to develop such concepts for years. Good, effective schools and departments have always recognised the idea of 'one opportunity'. All our pupils have one chance so we need to make sure that we address their problems and improve their life chances as quickly as possible. Once we recognise that pupils need extra help, it is important they get it quickly and that it effectively meets their needs. Getting the wider community on the school's side is vital. Selling the school's overall ethos is also about marketing the kinds of basic ideals that will help every aspect of the school be more effective:
- Tell parents what you want to do and ask their advice.
- Set up policy-forming groups that help create policies, for example on behaviour and anti-bullying.
- Use assemblies and lessons to put over wider concepts relating to behaviour and anti-bullying.

The I'm OK, you're OK school

It is never easy to balance the 'results' achieved by the school in terms of measurable outcomes, such as exams and tests, low rates of absenteeism etc., with the 'relationships' that exist between colleagues, teams, senior managers, departments etc. Adair (1983) suggests that there are three sets of needs that shift and change but which can directly influence how effective classroom teaching actually is. They are:
- jobs that need doing to achieve results
- the needs of the staff team/department team/whole-school team as a whole
- the needs of the individual within the staff/department/school

In order to resolve the problems raised by this kind of results/relationship issue, many whole schools and departments are organised and managed on a continuum similar to the one overleaf.

Autocratic	Paternalistic	Consultative	Democratic/collegial
(tell)	(sell)	(involve)	(share and co-determine)

You will find it interesting to see where you think your school or department is on the continuum because it is important to be at an appropriate place in order to be as successful as possible. In other words, if you are in the wrong place, whole-school attempts at creating effective teaching policies and effective classroom practice will be more difficult to implement. Read each of these descriptions of the points on the continuum and try and place your school or department.

- **Autocratic** — at this end of the continuum the strategy for organising the school is mostly 'telling'. Orders are given and they are expected to be followed. There is little or no teamwork and very few teams are part of the decision-making process. Individuals follow instructions rather than help create them.
- **Paternalistic** — there is a certain amount of dialogue and discussion within the school at this point on the continuum. Adults in school will talk to each other and there will be an attempt to persuade colleagues to follow certain ways of working. Any discussions either in teams or as part of whole-school meetings will not go beyond agreeing with the ideas that are being put forward from senior management or even just from the head teacher or head of department.
- **Consultative** — this will mean involving adults as part of the organisational culture of the school. They will be consulted about new ideas, changes in direction and new or different ways of working. This means that there is a move towards creating a whole-school ethos that involves all the adults who are affected by the decisions that are taken.
- **Democratic/collegial** — at this end of the continuum, the management and leadership processes that develop the school's ethos and aims involve consensus, and recognise that all adults working in the school who have delegated responsibilities must be able to play a part in and share and co-determine how the school functions.

If the school's position on the continuum is near to the democratic/collegial end, then there is a good chance of developing teaching strategies that everyone will follow and be happy with. Nevertheless, working alongside colleagues in a collegial way, even when it is accepted that this is the best way to develop whole-school/department strategies, is not easy. There will be colleagues who are more difficult to work with than others and also colleagues who will not find it easy to work together in a cohesive unit. If this happens it will mean that whole-school/department policies are not really whole-school or departmental at all and their effect will be dramatically reduced.

It is interesting to use the following 'OK and not OK' comparison (Montgomery, 1989). It gives four positions that colleagues can be in and which can lead to varying degrees of success when developing effective teaching policies.

Position 1   *I'm OK and everyone else is also OK* — all adults work well together and any changes and decisions that are related to managing specific issues, such as what are the most effective teaching styles etc., are relatively easy and straightforward.

Position 2   *I'm OK but you are far from OK* — decisions are taken by one person or group. This is not the way to develop a positive whole-school/department ethos. Only the minority taking the decisions are satisfied while the majority feel put upon and disgruntled.

Position 3   *I'm not OK but you are OK* — this is the position where there is an isolated individual or group who sees themselves as being left out or underachieving while everyone else seems to have taken certain decisions that mean that they are more successful and effective.

Position 4   *I'm not OK and you're not OK either* — if this is the situation in your school then no one is happy about how the school is moving forward and developing. In fact, no one will feel that they are actually getting anywhere. This is an intolerable position where any move towards trying to develop a positive teaching and learning ethos will be difficult if not impossible.

Both you and all your colleagues need to feel that you are playing a productive part in the school. Position 1 is obviously the position to aim for. If, after you have thought about your colleagues, you recognise that this is not the position that you are in, then you need to think about how to make sure that relationships are mended before any positive change can take place.

Developing consistently effective teaching

While it is true that you can have a direct effect on how effective the teaching and learning is inside your classroom, the ethos and efficiency of the whole school or whole department directly influences how successful you are. I suggest the following four attributes as contributing to a more positive, collaborative ethos:

1 Vision — good schools/departments will be aware of what is happening nationally and locally, and of their own successes. In both their own eyes and in those of the community will be reflected the 'vision' they project, which is able to meet the needs of their pupils but avoids parochialism and absorbs all that is best in current educational thinking.

2 **Thinking ahead** — all schools/departments have their own 'feelings' and 'attitudes' that set them apart and make them unique. The more positive everyone feels about what they are doing, the easier it is to 'think ahead', absorb changes and plan for the future.

3 **Trust and faith** — everyone needs to have faith in their colleagues and be able to trust them and value their professionalism and support.

4 **Imagination** — schools and departments with a clearly defined and obviously positive ethos have a kind of corporate enthusiasm and excitement about them. They become good at managing change and moving forwards because they are able to reduce anxiety, minimise stress and refuse to be complacent.

Three of the elements in attribute 4 — reducing anxiety, minimising stress and refusing to be complacent — are extremely important in recognising the pressures teachers are under and in creating an ethos that reduces these pressures. Look at your school/department in these terms and think carefully about whether its leaders and all your colleagues work together to create an ethos where there is as little stress as possible. Troman and Woods (2001) suggest that high burnout schools — not yours, I hope — tend to have an autocratic management style, goals that only lead to academic achievement and clearly defined hierarchies, with individuals working alone rather than in teams. In low burnout schools — hopefully yours — educational objectives are flexible, with less pressure for high standards and an organisational structure where teachers meet in both large and small groups to help take decisions and socialise.

The following summary can be used as a checklist for your school or department. If some of the following characteristics are absent in your school, you need to ask yourself what you can do and what should happen so that they can be developed.

- **Approachability** — issues such as classroom management, setting teaching objectives, managing classroom behaviour etc. are discussed out in the open so that you are able to approach and talk to other colleagues.
- **Openness** — good communication and open leadership with shared decisions and problems dealt with in a spirit of no blame and togetherness are all important.
- **Understanding** — teachers trust each other on an emotional, social and professional level.
- **Sharing** — there is a teacher culture of participation in shared values with more teamwork and less hierarchy.
- **Honesty** — problems are shared and not hidden away. This is especially important with sensitive issues related to monitoring and improving teaching and behaviour management, which can escalate into bigger problems if they are not tackled at an early stage.
- **Trust** — there is trust between colleagues, between teams and between leaders.

- **Knowledge and expertise** — the knowledge that all teachers have when considering the best and most effective teaching styles is shared. It is also important to recognise that good ideas come from all teachers — the newly qualified as well as the head of department, faculty head, deputy head or head teacher.
- **Values** — there is an emphasis on tolerance and mutual cooperation; such values will be reflected in relationships between teachers and pupils.
- **Realism** — there is a realistic approach to the kinds of problems that exist and the amount of work needed to solve them. Change takes place at a pace that can be sustained over a period of time.
- **Supporting others** — as teachers are trusted and supported by their colleagues, they are more willing to take risks that will make change work. If there is a collaborative culture that recognises strengths and weaknesses it is possible to develop lasting and sustained change.

The link between teaching, learning and behaviour

One of the reasons some whole schools/departments are more successful than others in developing consistently effective teaching is that they know what they want and how to get it. They also have positive policies that suggest what should happen in classrooms and what they actually mean by effective teaching and learning.

The following example of a whole school/department 'teaching and learning policy' can either be used as it is or modified to fit your particular circumstances. If you are going to use it or modify it, remember you will need to consider:
- whether it needs to be subject or department specific
- an agreed definition of teaching and learning
- how it fits into the ethos of the school/department
- how it meets the needs of both teachers and learners
- how the skills of teachers in school can be used to develop the policy

If you need to rewrite certain sections to meet your specific needs, it is important to:
- avoid too much jargon and make it easily accessible
- make sure it is clear, structured and easy to read as a whole and in sections
- link it, where possible, to other documents such as the behaviour policy, anti-bullying policy, the school effectiveness plan and the self-evaluation form (SEF)

While this kind of policy should be tightly structured to say exactly what is needed if there is to be a consistent approach, we shouldn't lose sight of the fact that we all need the freedom to be able to use our own enthusiasm, ideas, personal style and professional knowledge.

A teaching and learning policy

Introduction

The aim of this policy is to enable each pupil to reach his or her maximum potential. To do this, a peaceful environment has to be created in which tolerance, mutual cooperation and stability are encouraged so that each pupil can work productively, learn to make decisions, use his or her own judgement and cooperate courteously with others. As a school/department we are trying to achieve these high standards by responding professionally, sensitively and with care to the needs of all the pupils.

Aims

Teaching and learning within the school/department will:

- raise levels of attainment for all pupils
- develop confident, disciplined and enquiring learners
- foster a love of learning
- raise self-esteem
- increase personal responsibility
- ensure equal opportunities
- provide a safe and happy environment

Equal opportunities

All pupils will be given full access to the curriculum, including the national curriculum, and all staff will endeavour to help all pupils reach their full potential regardless of race, gender, class, ability, belief and culture.

What each teacher will aim to do

- Show good subject knowledge and understand how to present and develop their subject(s) in a manner that is appropriate to the age and ability of the pupils being taught.
- Show technical competence in teaching all aspects of their subject(s).
- Plan effectively to set clear objectives that all pupils understand.
- Challenge and inspire pupils and expect the most from them, so as to deepen their knowledge and understanding.
- Use a wide range of teaching methods that will enable each pupil to learn effectively.
- Insist on high standards of behaviour by managing pupils well.
- Use appropriate tests/exams and assessments to measure and compare progress.
- Use homework effectively to reinforce and extend what is learnt in school.

What is expected of each pupil?

Each teacher will expect each pupil to:

- acquire new knowledge and skills
- meet appropriate targets
- reach appropriate levels in both internal and external tests, assessments and examinations
- develop ideas
- increase their understanding
- apply intellectual, physical and creative effort to their work
- work at an appropriate pace
- show interest in their work
- sustain concentration appropriate to their age and ability
- think and learn for themselves
- understand what they are doing, how well they have done and how they can improve

Teacher expectations within lessons

In each lesson, each teacher will ensure that all pupils are:

- learning appropriate knowledge by acquiring or consolidating one or more of the key competencies that underpin their subject at an age-appropriate level
- receiving challenging work that they can understand and cope with successfully by using their existing intellectual, physical or creative effort
- receiving appropriate work that will help them achieve appropriate results in tests, assessments and examinations
- working productively at their optimum pace by remaining on-task
- being motivated by their teacher and other adults and pupils
- learning from their mistakes and asking for help when it is needed

Effective and successful learning

All teachers will recognise that learning is more effective when all pupils are:

- clear about what lesson objectives are
- engaged and informed by good teaching
- learning the right things for their age
- clear about what they are trying to achieve in terms of class and individual targets
- clear about how their work can improve
- able to understand what they are doing
- finding the tasks set demanding but achievable with sustained effort
- staying on-task and maintaining a good work rate
- well motivated

Effective teaching

All teachers will recognise that learning is less effective when pupils:

- are unsure about what work they are doing
- are doing purposeless activities
- find work too hard or too easy
- don't know how to improve
- are being made to work at too fast or too slow a pace
- are poorly motivated

Monitoring and evaluation

- This policy will be monitored once every 2 years.
- Teaching quality will be monitored at least once each year within the guidelines on confidentiality of the performance management policy and will include classroom observation.
- Subject managers will also monitor the quality of teaching in their subject.

The school/department will know that the policy is working when:

- Senior management and subject managers are satisfied that subjects are being taught well and that standards are being both maintained and raised.
- Realistic targets for pupil attainment are being met.
- All pupils reach realistic and appropriate levels of attainment.
- Whole-school/subject/department examination targets are being met.
- Ofsted judges that the quality of teaching is good or better throughout the school.

Behaviour and learning — a whole-school approach

The teaching and learning policy above emphasises the needs of individual pupils and their successes. It is also an inclusive policy, which should mean that there is the possibility of success for pupils of all abilities. Many pupils who are difficult to teach are marginalised and feel alienated from the curriculum and from the successes that are achieved by other pupils. This increases their sense of low self-esteem and increases the likelihood of disruptive and inappropriate behaviour. The policy also makes it clear that teaching and learning should be about motivation, increasing personal responsibility and providing a safe and secure environment where pupils cooperate courteously with others. In such an environment, where it is obvious that teachers care about each individual pupil, there should be less opportunity and less incentive for pupils not to learn. Ideally, the norm will be to learn, work hard and live by the rules. In other words, there is a strong link between attitude, teaching skills and achievement.

Each school must also have a 'behaviour and anti-bullying policy'. It is probably the umbrella under which most problems related to teaching, behaviour and learning are solved and it should demonstrate that no one will be working in isolation, but rather that there are rules and regulations to help everyone who finds particular pupils difficult. All schools need to have a behaviour policy but, of course, the amount of disruption and the number of problems that are related to unacceptable behaviour will vary from school to school, from teaching group to teaching group and teacher to teacher. Despite a positive whole-school/department ethos there will be some pupils who fail to meet the school's acceptable standards of behaviour. Some of the reasons for this will include:

- an inability to follow rules
- low self-esteem
- poor attendance
- special educational needs
- poor socialisation skills in the whole of the family, which will not support any kind of productive dialogue between home and school
- lack of parental support
- family circumstances such as divorce etc.

It would be useful to identify how many pupils you have in the whole school/department or in specific classes who fall within such categories. The more you have, the more difficult the task of maintaining and improving appropriate levels of behaviour will be, and the more teaching skills you will need to maintain and raise standards.

Activity 1.4 (p. 31) can be used to help identify individual pupils so that you can begin to take concerted and more consistent action to deal with any problems that are affecting the quality of your teaching and learning. Many of these unacceptable behaviours will lead to more frustration because they are barriers to success. The teaching and learning policy and any behaviour and anti-bullying policies can only suggest the broad outlines of how to deal with such pupils and it will be necessary to use teacher-specific skills. Pupils' attitudes are also very important. Their attitudes to teachers and to authority in general will be reasons for their possible low attainment. Pupils who behave well and relate successfully to other pupils and adults will be more interested and more able to concentrate during lessons. They will by and large achieve high standards. If a pupil has negative attitudes and relates badly to adults and other pupils, he/she is more likely to be a low achiever. The school or department's ethos, its teaching and learning policy, its behaviour and anti-bullying policy, and how teachers work within their own classrooms and teaching groups will have an influence on all the following barriers to learning:

- difficulty in participating in cooperative group work
- refusal to join in discussions

- unwillingness to persevere with set tasks
- lack of enthusiasm
- lack of pride
- inability to share resources
- inability to learn from mistakes
- inability to work without the direct supervision of an adult

Behaviour and teacher action

Activity 1.5 (p. 32) lists behaviour problems — there will be many more that you can add — followed by a checklist of possible teacher action. This is an important inventory at this stage for two reasons. First, the more behaviour problems there are, the more care needs to be taken in developing a detailed and effective behaviour policy. Second, if only a limited number of strategies are used, it will be useful to consider a wider range of possible actions. One way of using both checklists is for every teacher to complete them so that senior managers can analyse the results and think how they relate to whole-school/department teaching and learning policies and how teaching styles can be improved.

As well as helping you to develop an overview of effective teaching styles and how they are matched against preventing disruptive behaviour, the checklists can be used to help you to look at the profile of your classes and teaching groups and the tactics used. This will help you to focus on what specific strategies might be useful (suggestions are included in later sections).

Below is an example of a school or department's behaviour policy. It will be useful either as it stands or as a template to be modified to reflect your particular circumstances. It will also be useful to compare its aims with those of the example teaching and learning policy so that the two link together as closely as possible.

A behaviour and anti-bullying policy

Introduction

Our aim is to ensure that all pupils share a common educational experience within common boundaries of what is and is not appropriate behaviour.

1 We will create an ethos that is based on tolerance and mutual respect and is conducive to the learning and social development of all pupils.

2 The purpose of the behaviour and anti-bullying policy is to state clearly what our expectations of pupils' behaviour are and how we will deal with inappropriate behaviour in classrooms and around the school.

3 The policy needs to be continuously evaluated to see if we are meeting the high standards that we set ourselves.

Basic behaviour parameters

We will always aim to:

- respect each other
- cooperate with each other
- respect the rights and properties of others
- support each other if we are sad or upset
- be fair
- be tolerant
- provide a safe and peaceful environment

We make sure that this happens by:

- never hurting each other
- listening to each other
- making sure that there are no inappropriate loud noises in any area of the school
- not running or pushing through doors
- speaking to each other in a calm and polite way
- keeping our classrooms peaceful places to learn and work

We never accept:

- bullying
- racism
- sexism
- violence

Attendance

We expect:

- pupils to attend school every day
- pupils to arrive on time with all their appropriate equipment
- any absences or reasons for lateness to be reported on the same day

Parents can expect that:

- the school will keep a daily attendance record and will inform parents if the pattern of attendance of their child is causing concern
- pupils arriving late will be monitored and parents informed if there is a concern
- absences without authorisation will be checked with parents and if no good reason is given will be recorded as unauthorised
- persistent absences resulting in an unacceptable level of attendance will be discussed with parents and the school's educational social worker

Behaviour in lessons

We expect:

- pupils to arrive promptly for lessons — at the beginning of the school day and after breaks and lunchtime
- pupils to work sensibly in lessons to the best of their ability
- pupils not to prevent other pupils from learning or the teacher from teaching
- homework that is set to be competed on time and to an age- and ability-appropriate standard

Parents can expect:

- open evenings and target-setting meetings at least three times each year where general issues of performance, well-being and behaviour in the class-room will be discussed
- an annual report that has a section to inform parents about attitudes to work, behaviour, personal qualities etc.
- communication from school if it is felt that a pupil's behaviour is causing concern and that it would be helpful to share these concerns with parents
- pupils' work to be marked regularly, including homework
- pupils to be praised for good work and effort
- that if a child continues to be disruptive he/she will be dealt with in line with the school's hierarchy of behaviour management (Appendix 1)

Behaviour in the playground

What we expect:

- all pupils to be able to play peacefully and safely
- all pupils to be able to follow the guidelines in the basic behaviour parameters
- no pupil to behave violently, or to bully others in any way

Parents can expect:

- playgrounds to be supervised by teachers at break times and by lunchtime supervisors at lunchtime
- communication from school if their child is finding it difficult to socialise safely or is disruptive at break times
- that if a pupil causes persistent problems, he/she will be dealt with through the school's hierarchy of behaviour management (Appendix 1)

Behaviour at lunchtime

What we expect:

- all pupils to follow the guidelines in the basic behaviour parameters
- all pupils to follow the routines in the dining room safely, peacefully and quietly

Parents can expect:

- lunchtimes to be supervised by an appropriate number of lunchtime supervisors
- some teachers who are having lunch and preparing work to remain on site
- sanctions and reward systems to be operated by lunchtime supervisors
- supervisors to discuss individual pupils' behaviour with their form teacher or where necessary their year leader/head of department etc.
- if a child causes persistent problems, he/she will be dealt with through the school's hierarchy of behaviour management (Appendix 1) which may mean that he/she will be sent home for lunch for a fixed period of time

Violence and bullying

We expect:

- that there will be no physical violence between any members of the school community
- verbal bullying to be treated as seriously as physical violence
- persistent teasing to be treated seriously
- no discriminatory language to be used
- no member of the school community to be made unhappy by the actions of other pupils
- pupils to be able to move about the school and its grounds safely
- pupils to be able to move to and from school safely and that the standards of behaviour expected in school will be expected from pupils on their way to and from school

Parents can expect:

- to be be informed if their child is a victim of violence or bullying
- to be be informed if their child is being violent or is victimising others
- that there will be a full investigation of any serious incident and all those involved will be informed of the outcome
- that the school staff is a listening staff and a pupil's complaints of any relevant kind related to violence and/or bullying will be treated as a serious incident until proved otherwise
- that if they have concerns, a meeting will be arranged so that they will be listened to seriously and professionally
- all incidents of violence and/or bullying (Appendix 2) to be dealt with through the school's hierarchy of behaviour management (Appendix 1)

Monitoring and evaluation

- The policy will be evaluated every 2 years within a full staff meeting or as part of a training day.
- It will be monitored termly using a staff meeting to determine whether there are any areas of concern that might lead to changes being necessary in the way we approach a particular aspect of behaviour management.

- If the number of behaviour incidents at level 3 (Appendix 1) causes concern, changes to the policy and to the strategies within the hierarchy of behaviour management will have to be considered.

Appendix 1 Hierarchy of behaviour management

Pupils will be made aware that they will be rewarded for good work and good behaviour in a manner that is appropriate for their development. This will involve reward stickers, certificates, whole-school awards etc. Sanctions will operate if behaviour is inappropriate. If a child progresses through this hierarchy of behaviour management or begins at a high level, then special educational needs (SEN) procedures will need to be followed because such behaviour will fall into the SEN category of emotional and behavioural difficulty (EBD).

Stage 1

At this level one person, i.e. the form teacher, is dealing with an incident that has happened in isolation or a minor concern expressed by a parent.

- The teacher will talk to the pupil alone and make him/her aware of why his/her behaviour is inappropriate and what constitutes appropriate behaviour. If it involves another pupil or a group of pupils, their actions will be discussed with them.
- The most appropriate sanction at this level is to make it clear to the pupil that the teacher disapproves and explain why. If there has been an isolated but serious incident then some of the sanctions at Stage 2 will be appropriate.
- Lunchtime supervisors will be able to deal with most, if not all, minor issues of this kind at lunchtimes but will inform form tutors at the end of lunchtime so that they can follow up any relevant issues.
- Many areas within Stage 1 will involve general behaviour issues such as talking at inappropriate times, lack of politeness, saying something inappropriate, minor relationship problems etc. How to behave in such circumstances can be emphasised during tutor groups, year and whole-school assemblies.
- It is important to monitor individual pupils to determine whether certain incidents occur more than once, are resolved easily or begin to escalate.
- Appropriate written notes should be kept in a pupil's file by the form teacher and parents should be made aware of any more serious concerns.

Stage 2

At this stage, the form tutor is concerned that a pupil's attitude and behaviour is not responding to any of the approaches taken at Stage 1 and that there is persistent inappropriate behaviour.

- The pupil typically will not have responded to any action taken at Stage 1 and will have come to the attention of several adults.
- The form tutor should now be keeping notes of every occasion of inappropriate behaviour. These notes are to provide evidence of the incident (date and time of incident) and the action taken (who else was involved, whether the action taken was effective).
- Sanctions that should be used include: talking to the child as in Stage 1, other teachers (especially heads of year) talking to the child, time out of the classroom, letters of apology, reports to senior teachers, head of year and/or the head of department, deputy head teacher etc., completing work during breaks and lunchtime, withdrawal from breaks and lunchtime, exclusion from school during lunchtime.
- Behaviour logs should also be kept if this is felt to be appropriate as a means of formally recording behaviour over a period of time. The pupil and the pupil's parents will be informed that this is taking place and the form tutor will be responsible for keeping these notes.
- Incidents at Stage 2 will begin to involve other more senior teachers, although it will still be the form tutor or possibly the deputy/head of year who initiates the main focus of actions and discussions with parents.
- During the discussions with parents, all the school's strategies will be described and the parents will be asked about behaviour at home and any reasons that they can think of for the pupil's inappropriate behaviour. It will also be appropriate to indicate that the pupil may be placed on the school's SEN register for further support.

Stage 3

At this stage, because the patterns of inappropriate behaviour are persisting, the pupil will be placed on the school's SEN register.

- All the support and sanctions at Stages 1 and 2 will have been used and full discussions will have taken place with the pupil's parents.
- The special educational needs co-ordinator (SENCo) will observe the pupil, review all notes, introduce individual educational plans (IEPs) and set up meetings involving all relevant parties including parents.
- The pupil will be referred to an appropriate outside agency for support and after a maximum of three terms a decision will be made either to move the child back to Stage 2, continue at Stage 3, or move the child to Stage 4.

Stage 4

At this stage, the child's behaviour will be extremely difficult to deal with and exclusion may be a possibility.

- Exclusion has to take place according to national and local guidelines and must be done properly and thoroughly.

- A pupil who is excluded for either a fixed period of time or permanently does not have to go through all the previous stages. Sudden extremes of behaviour, such as totally unacceptable violence, can lead directly to exclusion.

Support for teachers and teaching assistants

Any system of managing behaviour relies on a whole-school/department approach where teachers know that there is support for their actions, both in praising and rewarding good behaviour and in operating appropriate sanctions. A supportive approach to stop disruptive and inappropriate behaviour will work best if the following applies:

- All newly appointed members of staff will have a mentor who will act as their first level of support and help them become familiar with the behaviour policy.
- Members of the same year team and other colleagues who have previously taught a particular pupil can offer valuable information about the management of an individual pupil's behaviour and particular classroom management problems.
- The SENCo will support colleagues with advice about persistent behaviour difficulties.
- The head of year and other senior colleagues will be available to discuss issues and offer support.
- All meetings with parents should now involve more than one teacher.

Appendix 2 Bullying

Bullying is the systematic victimisation of another person. It is to be taken seriously at all times and pupils should know (during incidents of bullying it should be clear to the victim as well as the victimiser) that it is being treated seriously.

Incidents of bullying can fall outside the hierarchy of behaviour management (Appendix 1) and can need instant and thorough action. However, it is important to make sure that everyone recognises that definitions of bullying can vary and are not always accurate.

- Distinctions have to be made between some common, unpleasant aspects of growing up and more serious behaviour.
- Action should not be taken at a high level for minor incidents or this will make dealing with very serious issues more difficult.
- All incidents should be acted on at an appropriate level and this will mean that in some cases relationship and friendship problems will, with careful monitoring, be allowed to run their natural course.
- It is important that pupils have free time when they are not directly supervised by an adult. Peer interaction is important for their development and all pupils need space to explore relationships, experiment with friendships, take decisions and make mistakes.

- Adult intervention at an inappropriate level will not help pupils prepare themselves for the time when they will have to manage their own relationships. A pupil who never learns how to cope with or resolve conflict may well have real problems as an adult.

What is bullying behaviour?

- It can be physical, verbal or just a series of looks.
- It can be overt or subtle intimidation.
- It is the wilful, conscious desire to hurt someone.
- It can be excluding a victim from enjoyable activities or from specific places in school.
- All bullying is aggression but all aggression is not bullying.
- It is the illegitimate use of power to hurt someone.
- Specific bullying behaviour will include: general name calling, teasing, racist taunting, homophobic name calling, texting and phoning inappropriately, taking money or possessions, stealing and threatening reprisals, damaging possessions, physical violence and rude, threatening and/or obscene gestures.

Who is the bully?

Bullies can be boys or girls. Some pupils become temporary bullies because of a traumatic event such as divorce, birth of a new baby, death in the family etc. Similarly, most of these events may help create a temporary victim.

Pupils who are found to be bullies usually like the feeling of power and often:
- feel insecure, inadequate and humiliated
- have been abused in some way
- are scapegoats and are bullied at home
- are under pressure at home to succeed at all costs
- have low self-esteem
- are encouraged by parents to overreact violently, to bear grudges and to adopt a hard, menacing attitude in their relationships with peers and adults

Both male and female bullies tend to have the following in common:
- They have assertive and aggressive attitudes over which they have little control.
- They lack empathy and can't imagine what their victim feels like.
- They lack guilt and rationalise that their victim somehow deserves to be bullied.
- They are usually bigger, stronger and older than their victim.
- They are impulsive with a strong need to dominate.
- They are usually associated with general anti-social behaviour and rule breaking.
- They are often aggressive towards parents and siblings.

Recognising victims and signs of bullying

Victims are usually vulnerable children, but teachers have to be alert to every child's complaint of bullying because it may be the case that assertive children are really complaining of relationship problems between a group of friends and that bullying is not the appropriate word to use. Particularly vulnerable are:

- pupils who are new to the school
- pupils who are different in speech, appearance and background
- pupils who suffer from low self-esteem
- those who demonstrate reactions such as tantrums or loss of control or who are very nervous or anxious

Recognising the signs displayed by victims

There are several signs that parents and teachers should be able to recognise that may indicate stress. It is important to bear in mind, however, that these signs could indicate a different cause. Victims may:

- be frightened of walking to and from school
- stay behind after school near to a teacher until other pupils have gone
- be unwilling to go to school
- ask to be taken to school and brought home
- begin to perform poorly in school work
- arrive home with property or clothes dirty or damaged
- arrive home hungry because lunch has been stolen or damaged
- have a poor appetite at home
- cry themselves to sleep
- have nightmares
- have unexplained bruises or scratches
- have possessions go missing at school
- ask for money or begin stealing money to take to school
- refuse to say what is wrong

Teachers should be able to link patterns of behaviour to cause and advise parents on what may be causing new and different patterns of behaviour and vice versa. It is important that teachers and parents are aware of and notice how pupils behave and whether their behaviour has changed.

Responses to and action against bullying: advice for teachers

First of all don't be shocked that it is happening, and don't blame yourself or your relationships with pupils or your teaching styles and methods of classroom management. Don't immediately think of ways of initiating draconian action. When bullying occurs action needs to be taken that is rapid, but also thoughtful and thorough.

Some immediate strategies include:

- Remaining calm — reacting loudly and emotionally may increase the bully's fun.
- Letting the bully and the victim know that you are taking the incident seriously.
- Removing the bully and making him/her wait in a quiet, safe place.
- Reassuring the victim and preventing him/her from blaming him/herself or feeling inadequate or foolish.
- Offering the victim immediate advice and support.
- Making it plain to the bully that you strongly disapprove of what he/she has done.
- Encouraging the bully to see the victim's point of view.
- If the victim is in agreement, setting up a bullying court where the victim with friends in support confront the bully and state exactly what he/she has done and what effect it has had.
- Reporting the incident to a senior teacher so that it can be followed up using the hierarchy of behaviour management (Appendix 1).

Some longer term issues include:

- Trying to think what triggered the incident and whether there are actions that could be taken to prevent further incidents.
- There may be whole-class and whole-school issues related to the incident which could be followed up in assemblies, tutor groups, citizenship, PSHE etc.
- There may be issues related to how well the 'play' areas and school grounds are being supervised and changes may need to be made.

Skills summary

This chapter has concentrated on the idea that every teacher has to be able to exercise their professional expertise. However, they need to be able to do this within the structures and certainties of a positive whole-school or department ethos. This can be a relatively elusive concept because it is concerned with the characteristics of the school/department as a socially cohesive organisation. It is also about the 'feelings' and 'vibrations' given off by the school or department and the positive ways, such as coherent teaching, learning and behaviour policies, that are used to promote consistent ways of working. One fundamental issue is that you should never feel that you are working alone. Your successes should be shared and celebrated and your effective strategies and techniques used by everyone. Similarly, your problems need to be solved in a supportive way by colleagues who are determined to work alongside you to raise standards.

Activity 1.1

What makes a teacher 'good' and what makes a teacher 'bad'

Think of two teachers about whom you have strong memories. One of them should be someone you felt was a 'good' teacher and the other a 'bad' teacher. Use the boxes to write down some of your reasons. In other words, what did the teachers actually do that made them 'good' or 'bad'?

'Good' teacher
'Bad' teacher

With the same two teachers in mind, think about the following questions:
- Did most pupils dislike the 'bad' teacher or was it just a personal dislike?
- What did this teacher do or fail to do that caused such dislike?
- Did you ever feel that you learned anything worthwhile from the 'bad' teacher?
- If you didn't learn anything, why not?
- Did most people like the good teacher?
- If so, why was he/she so well liked?
- Did you learn more from this teacher than from the 'bad' teacher?
- If so, why?

It should be possible for you to use this information. It may sound simplistic but you will want to behave like the 'good' and not like the 'bad' teacher. With this in mind, write down what you want to do as a teacher — and, of course, what you don't want to do.

What I will do to teach in a positive and 'good' way
What I won't do that would make me seem like a 'bad' teacher

Activity 1.2

Self-recognition chart

You are going to look at yourself and make decisions about the following:
- how you *really* feel when you are working (R)
- how you would *ideally* like to feel when you are working (I)

To complete the chart, write 'R' for how you *really* feel on the scale between each pair of characteristics, e.g. if you usually feel quite attractive:

Attractive _____R_____ Unattractive

Finish the whole list before going on to the next stage.

Now rate yourself according to how you would *ideally* (I) like to be. For example, you really (R) feel quite unintelligent a lot of the time but would ideally (I) like colleagues to think of you as very intelligent.

Intelligent _____I_____R_____ Unintelligent

Self-recognition chart

Attractive	_____	Unattractive
Active	_____	Passive
Quiet	_____	Loud
Fair	_____	Unfair
Kind	_____	Unkind
Happy	_____	Sad
Intelligent	_____	Unintelligent
Introverted	_____	Extroverted
Humble	_____	Boastful
Stressed	_____	Relaxed
Strong	_____	Weak
Trusting	_____	Sceptical

Independent   _____   Conforming

Powerful   _____   Weak

Sensitive   _____   Insensitive

Polite   _____   Impolite

Hard-working   _____   Lazy

Generous   _____   Mean

Gregarious   _____   Solitary

Tolerant   _____   Intolerant

Friendly   _____   Unfriendly

Interesting   _____   Boring

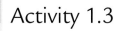

Activity 1.3

Staff relationship grid

You are going to place each member of your school's or department's staff on the staff relationship grid bearing in mind:

- how you feel they rate your professional expertise
- how much you think they like you

Look at the example shown on the staff relationship grid below. You think that Mr X doesn't like you very much (score 2) but he thinks you are quite good in terms of professional competence (score 8). You think Mrs Y likes you as a person (score 9) but disagrees with you about how to teach and deal with pupils (score 3).

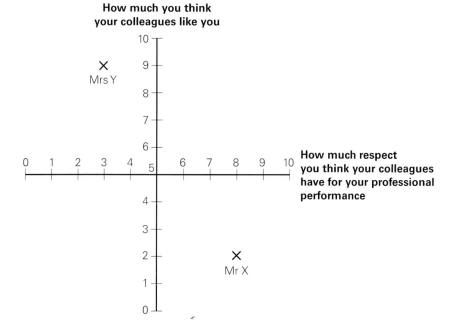

Now place each of your colleagues on the blank staff relationship grid overleaf.

Staff relationship grid

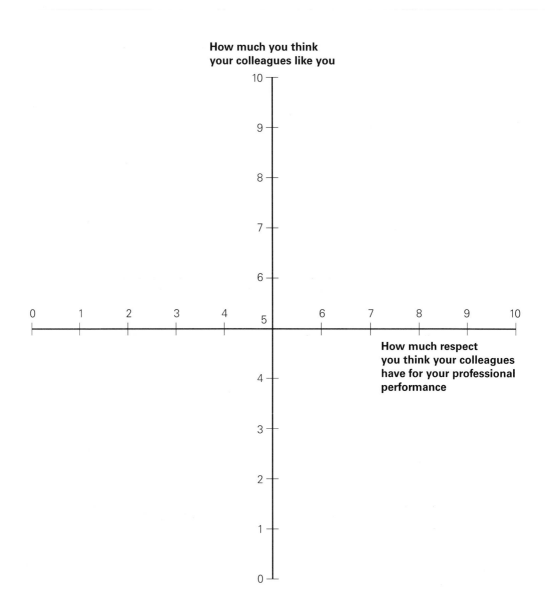

**How much you think
your colleagues like you**

**How much respect
you think your colleagues
have for your professional
performance**

Activity 1.4

Behaviours that can disrupt teaching

This activity can help to identify disruptive pupils. Read each 'behaviour' example and write down the names of pupils who behave in this way. When you have finished, and if it is helpful, share this information with colleagues.

Slow in settling to any task
Routinely making little or no effort and copying other pupils' work
Deliberately distracting other pupils by talking and moving round the room etc.
Easily distracted by other pupils
Unable to meet deadlines such as finishing work in the classroom and completing homework
Talking when they should be listening
Poor response to praise
Working to a superficial level
Serious inappropriate behaviour such as violence, obscene language and a refusal to follow instructions
Problems related to SEN issues such as autism, Asperger's syndrome, ADHD etc.

Activity 1.5

Matching behaviour with action

1 List of behaviour issues

Tick all of the boxes below that apply to members of your teaching group. If you want to follow on from **Activity 1.4**, write down pupils' names alongside their behaviour.

Moodiness ☐ _____

Irritability ☐ _____

Over anxiousness ☐ _____

Fear of failure ☐ _____

Stuttering ☐ _____

Nervous twitches ☐ _____

Sad and miserable ☐ _____

Fussing with trivial complaints ☐ _____

Vulnerability and victim of bullying ☐ _____

Frequent tears ☐ _____

Immature and inappropriate
leisure activities ☐ _____

Social isolation ☐ _____

Excessively quiet ☐ _____

Talk of suicide ☐ _____

Attention seeking ☐ _____

Aggressive attitude ☐ _____

Hitting other pupils ☐ _____

Self-mutilation ☐ _____

Severe temper ☐ _____

Cheekiness ☐ _____

Frequent silliness ☐ _____

Over activity ☐ _____

Frequent absences ☐ _____

Stealing ☐ _____

Destructiveness with property ☐ _____

Bullying ☐ _____

Getting others into trouble ☐ _____

Calling out ☐ _____

Moving around the room ☐ _____

2 Action taken by the teacher

Tick each of the possible actions that you use in your classroom. To be more specific, write down pupils' names alongside actions that actually work.

Remember, this information will be useful if it is shared with colleagues who need to know what individual pupils do and the kind of teacher action that stops them doing it.

Overlook and ignore the inappropriate behaviour ☐ _____

Remind the pupil that you disapprove ☐ _____

Discuss the problem with the pupil ☐ _____

Reprimand the pupil privately ☐ _____

Reprimand the pupil in front of the group ☐ _____

Alter the seating arrangements in the group ☐ _____

Reorganise the way the group is taught ☐ _____

Check that there is a good match between the pupil's ability and the work set ☐ _____

Look at the pupil's file for family and medical reasons ☐ _____

Keep the pupil in at break ☐ _____

Give the pupil extra work ☐ _____

Deprive the pupil of special privileges ☐ _____

Send the pupil out of the room ☐ _____

Send the pupil to another teacher ☐ _____

Arrange a detention ☐ _____

Send the pupil to the head of department/senior teacher/head of year or deputy etc. ☐ _____

Use the pupil's name more frequently ☐ _____

Smile at the pupil more often ☐ _____

Notice the pupil more often outside the classroom ☐ _____

Praise desirable behaviour ☐ _____

Praise small improvements in the pupil's work ☐ _____

Arrange for a teaching assistant to work with the pupil ☐ _____

Use behaviour contracts and daily behaviour charts ☐ _____

Arrange to talk to the pupil's parents ☐ _____

Encourage peers to help the pupil ☐ _____

Improve the pupil's self-esteem by giving responsibilities ☐ _____

2 Whole-school ideas for effective teaching and learning

This chapter continues the whole-school/department theme and reinforces the view that you need the full support of colleagues as well as systems and structures in place that make all your skills and strategies easier to use. Some of the suggestions may apply more to younger secondary pupils. Some, like the first suggestion — 'the 3-metre rule' — can apply to everyone, all pupils and all staff.

The 3-metre rule

Many of the problems that prevent teaching and learning from taking place are caused by pupils with low self-esteem. Lawrence (2001) suggests that:

> A vast body of evidence has accumulated showing a positive correlation between self-esteem, achievement and behaviour...there is clear evidence that relationships between teachers and students can be either conducive to the enhancement of high self-esteem or conducive towards reducing self-esteem. (p. 43)

Raising self-esteem is important at a whole-school level as well as in the classroom (see 'Reducing stress, raising self-esteem and building confidence', Chapter 6 pp. 105–8) and anything that can have an immediate impact is worth trying. This idea encourages both adults and pupils to relate positively to each other. The rule is that if you pass someone at a distance of 3 metres or less, you acknowledge them by smiling or saying hello or something equally positive. This applies equally to pupils and teachers. It helps create a happier more positive environment with friendlier relationships. It also makes pupils feel more valued because more people are speaking to them in more positive ways.

No put-downs

Having a no put-downs policy sounds simple but is more difficult to put in place than the 3-metre rule. It is worth trying because, in aiming to make the school and the classrooms 'put-down' free, you are making it clear that no one is allowed to sneer at anyone else or attempt to score points or minimise anyone's contribution to a lesson or an activity. It works best if it is introduced at the younger end of the school and it is often a good way to help raise boys' achievement and maximise their contribution to lessons, because boys often feel less confident when answering questions and taking part in discussions. It also works best alongside a philosophy of 'no blame', where blame is not attached to a person in a belittling way and where problems are there to be solved rather than hung round an individual's neck. Once pupils understand what 'put-downs' are and that they are not allowed, they usually take part with enthusiasm because they will recognise that it allows each of them to make mistakes without ridicule from either a misguided teacher — because it applies equally to adults — or any of their peers.

Essential rules and leisure activities

Essential rules are about setting clear boundaries and straightforward, easily recognised standards of what is acceptable and unacceptable. Once again, they are part of a whole-school strategy as success will depend on the rules being maintained at *all* times by *all* adults. As with the 3-metre rule, they may work best if they are introduced to younger pupils and then used consistently as this particular year group moves through the school. But why not go for gold and use these ideas for all pupils of whatever age, remembering that it is not suffi-cient just to display your rules on your tutor room walls; they need to be modelled throughout the school.

As a very positive whole-school system, using essential rules empowers pupils. To a certain extent, they take some control over their own behaviour. It also begins with the positive assumption that everyone is capable of working without breaking essential rules. It places responsibility in the hands of individual pupils and concentrates on three main categories:

- respecting ourselves
- respecting others
- respecting our own and other peoples' possessions

First of all there should be a meeting to agree a list of common rules that all teachers feel the school or their department needs. These are developed by the staff as a whole and will include such important statements as:

- no violence in the classroom
- no loud noises or calling out
- no interfering with other pupils' work
- no running
- no damaging property
- no name calling

Each teacher needs to take these agreed whole-school rules back to their tutor group. Ideally there should be no more than ten rules — a maximum of six would be ideal. The rules that are devised need to be age appropriate and worded so that each pupil in the tutor group understands them.

Once the essential rules have been established, write them down and display them prominently in your tutor room. After pupils have become familiar with them over a period of a few days, with all the necessary reminders, it is time to link them to 'leisure activities' as a whole-school concept. Here's how it works.

On the first Monday of an agreed week form tutors will tell their pupils that on Friday afternoon everybody can have 30–45 minutes with a choice of different activities. This is leisure time. These activities need to be the kinds of things that pupils like doing — so they need to be age related and can include such activities as: watching a DVD, listening to their own music, doing homework, doing revision, drawing, painting etc. If there are talented teaching assistants available or volunteer parents, maybe wider activities can be introduced.

The assumption you make, and which is communicated to each pupil, is that everyone deserves leisure time, everyone will want it and everyone will get it as they are all capable of following the essential rules, because — and here is the stick that goes alongside the leisure-time carrot — it is the responsibility of every pupil to keep the essential rules. If a pupil breaks any of them they will miss a specified amount of leisure time. Each time an essential rule is broken, leisure time is lost. Pupils are responsible for their own actions and they begin to see the consequences of their behaviour and the effect their behaviour has. Some schools develop a system where it is possible to earn back leisure time. If this system is adopted, what a pupil has to do to earn back lost time must be a task or a pattern of behaviour that is hard to achieve and that requires a significant amount of effort, otherwise some pupils will see losing time as a slight hiccup rather than as something that is detrimental and serious.

During leisure time itself, those pupils who have lost part or all of it must not take part in any of the activities or be given anything to do that can be seen as interesting or worthwhile. Sitting them in the middle of the activities with absolutely nothing to do so that they can see other pupils having a good time is the best sanction. As soon as their time out has finished, they immediately join in with the activity of their choice. On the other hand, it may be more practical to isolate pupils who have lost time from different tutor groups in one place where they can be supervised together and given some kind of work to do as a punishment.

Using mediators

A major part of using rules, sanctions and rewards such as essential rules and leisure time is to make sure that mutual respect and maintaining self-esteem are high priorities. Once there are whole-school or department rules and strategies in place, the next step is to move on to what makes each pupil a better person and how to encourage pupils to understand how they can resolve their own conflict. This is almost a move towards developing citizenship, and partly rejects retribution and punishment (although there must still be a place for this) in favour of more creative ways of resolving behaviour issues. A strategy known as restorative justice uses peer mediators and is a useful tool in the battle against inappropriate attitudes, poor behaviour and social issues, such as friendship problems and bullying, for the following reasons:

- It allows the pupils involved to be heard and in many cases this results in an apology that can be all that is required to resolve a difficult situation.
- It empowers pupils to begin to articulate their problems and to move forwards by being encouraged to make their own suggestions and ideas.
- It tries to reach solutions that everybody agrees with, which means that pupils are more likely to feel that they 'own' the solutions rather than having sanctions etc. imposed on them.
- If there is a trained team of mediators in school it means that they can be used quickly so that disagreements etc. can be tackled before they escalate.

However, it is a waste of time training and using older pupils as mediators unless your school has the appropriate ethos. This is because the technique works best when pupils know exactly what restorative justice entails, are willing to take part because they understand how it will work and that relationships in school are pitched in a way that encourages working together cooperatively. **Activity 2.1** (p. 48) suggests the kind of checklist that needs to be completed before you consider using mediation techniques. Once you have considered each of the statements, it is important to think what the whole school or department needs to do next if you feel that this is a way forward in resolving the kinds of pupil conflict you are regularly faced with. **Activity 2.2** (p. 49) outlines the requirements of each of the three stages for adopting this approach. Once again it suggests very clearly the need for the school or department team to work together in order to make positive changes.

If mediation seems like a good idea, training for mediators is essential and it is probably best to find an expert. Some schools may be lucky and have teachers who are able to do this but others may have to use an outside trainer. If you are looking for pupils to train as mediators it will be important that they all have the following basic but invaluable characteristics:

- friendly
- thoughtful
- caring
- confidential

- helpful
- understanding
- fair

They will also need to be willing to take part and want to work with other pupils because they care about conflict situations and bad behaviour and want to play a part in minimising it. The website www.leaplinx.com/youth/ymn.htm suggests that peer mediation is all about:

- a way of communicating where pupils who are in disagreement with each other actually begin to talk to each other
- using mediation skills to help pupils work out their own difficulties
- allowing pupils in conflict to find their own answers to their problems rather than being given solutions
- providing a safe and secure opportunity for both pupils in a dispute to tell their side of the story and be taken seriously
- looking to the future to prevent the same kind of conflict happening again

It also suggests that peer mediation should be taken seriously because it:

- creates a calmer school environment
- helps to combat bullying and racial harassment
- helps pupils to deal with stresses at home and at school
- reduces violence

If peer mediation does do this, then it is important to look at it carefully as a whole-school/department strategy and ask seriously whether it should be one of the ideas that you would like to use.

Music and meditation

Creating a gentle, calm and peaceful atmosphere is every school's aim. Playing Mozart, for example, in corridors and cloakrooms, is reputed to have a calming effect on behaviour and improve the mood as well as increasing memory capacity. This may be because the music itself affects moods. However, it may also be that it is so very far removed from what most pupils normally listen to that they will be far too embarrassed to relate to it in any way.

Some schools are using meditation alongside music as a calming influence and as a way of alleviating the kind of mental stress that can lead to inappropriate and negative attitudes. There are suggestions that daily meditation can raise standards, allow pupils to take charge of their own learning, improve confidence and introduce a way of stilling the forces of hyperactivity. The theory is that there are links between how the brain works creatively and the deep silence of meditation. Schools using meditation think that meditation develops the use of positive and productive mental energy so that pupils are not constantly dissipating energy and using it in a negative and destructive way.

Some anecdotal studies in the USA are taking these views even further and suggesting that meditation can manage serious conditions such as attention deficit and hyperactivity disorder (ADHD). If you have someone who could develop meditation or are willing to 'buy in' someone to lead sessions with pupils, it may be worth trying just so that it can help pupils to slow down for a few minutes in their busy, stressful and competitive days as well as controlling their emotions and reducing their potential for angry responses.

Using school councils

There has been a significant growth in the number of schools giving pupils a voice in their decision-making processes. This has been recognised as important by Ofsted who sees the presence of a school council as a key indicator of a successful school because a school council is able to:

- improve academic performance
- reduce bullying and vandalism
- reduce school exclusions
- improve pupil–pupil relations and teacher–pupil relations
- develop responsible attitudes and better behaviour
- give pupils hands-on experience of wider school issues such as the curriculum, PSHE, democracy and citizenship
- instil in pupils feelings of belonging to the school, being part of the decision-making process, developing listening skills and improving self-confidence

There are more suggestions related to creating and running school councils on www.schoolcouncils.org and on the Standards Site at www.standards.dfes.gov.uk.

Decisions taken by the school council must move beyond improving the tuck shop and toilets, and the council itself should not be just a symbolic and adult-manipulated institution. Councils do, however, need to be built up from the bottom and start with relatively small issues because they are more likely to be rapidly successful, rather than being frustrated by not being able to make huge instant changes.

School councils are, of course, a whole-school issue and should be started and developed by being given whole-school publicity through assemblies and through being part of each pupil's PSHE and citizenship lessons. Usually, each tutor group sends representatives to the school council. This is an important starting point — getting this right will make the school council function more successfully. Mini tutor group councils that give advice and suggest issues to the full school council representatives should be:

- inclusive and structured forums for discussion and decision-making
- a means for pupils to raise issues and concerns
- a means where the school council gets to consult all pupils

This third point is significant. The school council will only promote change and share whole-school concerns if the representatives from each tutor group really do reflect the views of the pupils in them and have the skills to resolve problems. To do this they need to be trained in how committees are structured and how they work and take decisions. One of the key skills for school council representatives is that of mediation. The skills involved include:

- being able to listen to both sides
- not taking sides but having an impartial view
- helping others to solve problems rather than solving problems for them

Many local authorities recognise the importance of school councils and are able to offer courses for teachers who will then be able to train children effectively. The mark of its success, of course, will be whether the school council is able to take decisions to solve problems that are important to the pupils, and whether this kind of participation does raise standards and create an ethos where negative attitudes are not the norm and do not influence how the school operates in terms of teaching and learning.

Some questions to ask in terms of whether your school council is effective include:

- Are your tutor-group representatives elected properly?
- Do they have opportunities to report back what happened at the school council meeting?
- Do all pupils have the opportunity to discuss school council issues either in the tutor group or as part of the full school council?
- Are meetings held often enough?
- Are the school council officers, i.e. chairperson, secretary, treasurer etc. elected annually?
- Do the school council members listen to each other properly?
- Are all the staff, i.e. teachers, teaching assistants and administrative staff, supportive?
- Does the school council have a budget?
- Are the tutor-group representatives and full council officers trained?
- Are there too many class representatives — or too few?
- Are the meetings held at the right time and in the right place?

At the meetings:

- Are the agendas short, relevant and interesting?
- Do all representatives have copies of the agenda well before the meeting?
- Are the meetings the right length?

- Is there an action plan for decisions or are teachers left to sort it out?
- Are exciting changes planned or is it all rather humdrum and low key?
- Can issues that really trouble pupils on a daily basis be dealt with swiftly?

Improving the working environment

There are many schools throughout the country which are taking a radical look at the kinds of changes and developments that will modify and improve the whole-school ethos. The most effective of these developments share the idea that the better the working environment, the more pupils will enjoy being in it, and the more they enjoy being there, the more positive their attitude will be to learning and good behaviour. Some of the suggestions might already be in place in your school. They include:

- **Breakfast clubs** — these can provide a healthy start to the day and can be expanded as havens of early morning security. With adult volunteers they can be developed into homework clubs or clubs for all kinds of other leisure pursuits that can take place before school starts.
- **Mid-morning snacks** — for all pupils, and especially those with behaviour and attitude problems, additive and sugar-free food is essential. A mid-morning snack of, for example, toast, vegetables, fruit and smoothies can help.
- **School meals** — this is currently an important national issue which perhaps needs a more dictatorial stance. Obesity, short-term and long-term ill health and a much shorter life span are all a direct consequence of what we eat, and yet we still allow pupils in schools to eat and drink foods that contribute to all these problems. There needs to be a dramatic and sustained move towards healthy eating that will support learning, positive attitudes and behaviour management, reduce obesity and improve fitness. Foods need to be as free from additives, fat and salt as possible, unprocessed and organic with water rather than coloured fizzy drinks being the only drink allowed.
- **Improving the school environment** — schools needs to be as attractive as possible. There should be superb displays of pupils' work, which they take great pride in. Some displays, especially of art work, could be improved by using high-quality frames. Carpets could be laid, soft furnishings and comfortable chairs provided in shared areas. The temperature should be neither too hot nor too cold. There is also a suggestion that plants in the classroom improve the air quality because without them the high levels of carbon dioxide can affect many pupils' capacity to learn. In crowded classrooms, the recommended level of carbon dioxide can be exceeded by 500%. More plants will reduce this as will opening windows and making sure that there is a healthy flow of fresh air.
- **Sports clubs** — these can help all pupils attain a certain level of fitness and can be of considerable benefit to pupils who are able to succeed at something that is not necessarily seen as 'academic'. Some schools hire coaches at lunchtimes to run clubs, which takes the pressure off lunchtime supervisors by reducing

the number of pupils in the playground and possibly freeing up more space for them. After-school clubs and activities can improve teachers' skills as well as those of pupils. As well as the usual team games such as football, hockey, rounders, netball and cricket, it is important to cater for individual sports such as martial arts and quieter ones such as chess and other table-top games.

Understanding the barriers to learning

The Elton Report (1989) uses the phrase 'school atmosphere' (p. 89) and emphasises that there are 'differences in a school's feel or atmosphere' (p. 88) and that 'perhaps the most important characteristics of schools with a positive atmosphere is that pupils, teachers and school staff feel that they are known and valued members of the school community' (p. 90). It goes on to suggest that schools can have a positive or a negative atmosphere and that those with a negative atmosphere will suffer more from barriers to good behaviour and learning — such as poor attitudes, inability to concentrate and low parental support — than those with a positive atmosphere. Symptoms that suggest a negative atmosphere, and that themselves will lead to low expectations and poor standards, include:

- widespread litter
- long-standing graffiti
- teachers starting lessons late and finishing early
- teachers ignoring incidents outside the classroom and in the playground
- the use of inappropriate punishment and rewards

So far, Chapter 1 and the early parts of this chapter have concentrated on how the school or department's policies, ethos and strategies can affect standards at all levels but, of course, pupils create their own barriers to high achievement. They may not perform as well as they should and you will have to look at whether you have set the most appropriate targets or whether you need to modify your planning and differentiation etc. There will also be general, whole-school and whole-department reasons that will have to be tackled by all your colleagues rather than you on your own. Some of the 'general' reasons for low achievement that everyone will have to face up to include:

- pupils with special needs
- poor attendance
- high incidences of lateness
- an inability to accept rules
- poor socialisation skills so that there is often conflict at home, with teachers and with peers
- lack of parental support, even rejection by parents of what the school and the education system can offer

- family changes such as divorce, separation or death in the family
- lack of participation in anything that the school offers, including after-school clubs and sports activities

You will recognise many of these barriers and understand that while some may prove to be intractable, others can be influenced by the positive action of the school and other agencies which can cooperate to assist families and individuals to succeed. The *Every Child Matters* agenda, for example, should help bring together support teams using educational psychologists, educational welfare officers, social workers, health workers and the police. To some extent, some of the barriers are out of your hands. For example, a difficult family separation that affects learning and attitudes can occur suddenly and be hard to manage. A death in the family can be totally unexpected but have a devastating effect on a pupil's learning. Such incidents cannot be planned for and you will have to deal with them as best you can within the supportive framework of the school.

The attitude of pupils to learning can often be more powerful than any innate ability and measurable intelligence, and can determine, to a greater degree, how they will react to and benefit from your teaching. You will have to build on your pupils' positive attitudes and work hard to eliminate — or at least minimise and marginalise — those that are negative so that they will be interested in the work that they are asked to do, be able to sustain concentration and will be involved in tasks set by you and tasks that they set themselves. Model pupils can and should be used as examples to pupils with less well-developed attitudes. In fact, one of the main aims of the whole school or department should be to promote these kinds of attitudes because negative attitudes, if they are allowed to persist, will be accepted by pupils and teachers and will start dominating the ethos and 'atmosphere' of the school or department. If this is allowed to happen, they will be difficult to overcome and it is unlikely that pupils with negative attitudes will benefit from the curriculum and how it is taught because they will show:

- unwillingness to apply themselves to tasks
- refusal to join in discussions
- unwillingness to persevere to complete tasks or to solve difficult problems
- obvious lack of enthusiasm
- lack of pride in any of their work
- difficulty in participating in cooperative learning
- inability to share resources, including their own and those belonging to the school
- inability to learn from their mistakes
- aversion to making mistakes but will be quick to laugh at the mistakes of others
- inability to work without the direct supervision of a teacher

Teachers are usually skilled in minimising negative attitudes but are not always their own best publicists when it comes to stating what it is that they actually do. Schon (1983) raises an interesting point — which is worth bearing in mind when you are trying to articulate your ideas to colleagues — by describing the skilled actions of teachers as 'knowledge in action'. What he meant was that teachers can often demonstrate in action what they are doing but find it difficult to verbalise or describe. It is a pity that teachers cannot just reel off all the skills, strategies and tactics they are using, because schools do make a difference to pupils both academically and socially.

If you work in a deprived area, you will find that many pupils have poor role models at home, whose behaviour and attitudes may be of the kind that the school is trying to prevent. Verbal and physical aggression, for example, can be more frequent, so trying to involve parents more in what is happening in school is essential. This in itself will be more difficult, because many parents in this situation are more likely to have had bad experiences and little success during their own school life and do not find it easy to take part in school events. Schools can turn spare rooms into comfortable and welcoming parents' rooms with a crèche and coffee, tea and biscuits. There is also nothing better for changing pupils' attitudes from negative to positive — at least in the short term — than having the embarrassment factor of parents close at hand or even in the classroom. Health visitors are useful for talking to parents in a non-threatening way about positive parenting with tips about the kinds of supportive discipline that they can use at home. In fact, helping parents realise how much influence they have and how this needs to be positive rather than negative is an important part of reducing negative attitudes. For example, a parent's feelings of stress, sadness, anxiety, anger, frustration and tiredness will only serve to increase their child's level of inattentiveness and hyperactivity. This is obvious when it is thought through, because the most important issues in many pupils' lives will not be whether to be more positive in the classroom, to learn more or not to hit someone who has annoyed them, but whether their mother or father will be in a good mood or a bad one when they get home. If schools can help parents feel better about each other and be more energetic, confident and happy, it will have a positive effect on pupils, hopefully raising their self-esteem and helping them to overcome their own behaviour problems.

The right food and drink

Many schools are taking a serious look at the link between the capacity to learn, raised standards and what children eat and drink. An outright ban on sweets, crisps and fizzy drinks is becoming more widespread and is part of a wider, national issue. The Food in Schools (FiS) programme introduced by the

Department of Health and DfES has been prompted by concerns over the rising levels of childhood obesity and low levels of fitness, but many teachers also see this initiative as playing a key role in raising educational standards. You may be working in a school that is moving forwards on healthy eating and making what are obviously important changes. If this is the case, there are some key figures and statistics that might persuade reluctant colleagues and parents to move more quickly. The FiS website, www.wiredforhealth.gov.uk, suggests that schools working towards the healthy eating strand of the National Healthy School Standard need to take account of the following:

- 37% of pupils said they would select healthy foods at school if there was a better choice available and 18% wanted the taste of the healthy food options at school to be improved.
- 8% of pupils have nothing to eat before school and this rises to 18% for 15–16-year-olds and 20% for 15–16-year-old girls.
- In a typical week, one in five pupils will eat no fruit at all.
- It is estimated that 15% of all 15-year-olds are obese.
- Nine out of ten pupils are taking food to school that contains too much sugar, salt and saturated fat.
- When we are thirsty, mental performance deteriorates by 10%.
- 58% of pupils would like to be taught to cook at school.

Common food additives, colourings and preservatives can have a significant effect on some pupils' behaviour and their ability to learn — including increasing the likelihood of tantrums, violence, mood swings and hyperactivity, which will make it difficult for them to be taught effectively and prevents teachers working success-fully with other pupils. *The Food Magazine* (October 2002) summarises the conclu-sions of new studies to suggest that if certain additives continue to be allowed there is the risk of 'continuing behavioural difficulties including the transition to conduct disorder and educational difficulties'. It quotes statistics to the effect that if these additives were banned and removed from food, the rate of hyperactivity, for example, would go down from 1 in 6 to 1 in 17, and this at a time when it is estimated that 38% of the kinds of snacks and drinks aimed at young people contain all kinds of common additives. Healthier alternatives need to be provided through breakfasts, snacks and school meals.

Drinking water needs to be readily available because it is now thought to affect health, learning and behaviour in the following ways:

- Drinking water at regular intervals throughout the day is an important way of protecting health and contributing to well-being.
- Drinking an adequate intake of water can help prevent short-term and long-term health problems including headaches, bladder and bowel problems and cancer.

- Water is a much healthier drink than soft artificial drinks, which may be high in additives, sugar and caffeine.
- Mental performance is improved by frequent intakes of small amounts of water.
- When we are thirsty – which is the first sign of dehydration – mental performance deteriorates by 10%.
- Pupils concentrate better when they are not distracted by feelings of dehydration, i.e. thirst, tiredness and irritability.

The recommended daily amount of water for 10–13 year olds is two pints of fluid a day and six pints if they are exercising or it is hot. Dehydrated pupils who are lethargic and irritable will be unable to learn and the chances are they will be less amenable to normal positive school and classroom routines.

Involving parents

The importance of involving parents in the adoption of the positive ethos of a school is crucial. It is equally important to try to influence how parents treat their children at home. For example, the way parents handle conflict has a huge effect upon their children's emotional behaviour and how they relate to other people. Young people who are constantly exposed to serious conflict are less likely to learn as effectively as those who are not. Schools can run courses on how to discipline pupils because the style of parental discipline will significantly affect how pupils behave at school in terms of their inability to control their immediate impulses, their belief that all authority is against them and low self-esteem. Parents who are inconsistent, overbearing and arbitrary, for example, can create conflict and are often unsuccessful in their attempts to control their children. Those parents who are generally firm but fair and who trust their children have fewer conflicts and their children are less likely to get into trouble in school.

Parents and their children are the school's clients and need to be able to understand what the school is actually doing in creating the kind of positive and supportive ethos where conflict is at a minimum and where every child is happy, secure and able to learn to their maximum ability. **Activity 2.3** (p. 50) suggests some questions that can be put to parents and pupils and teachers.

An effective school is one that is effective for everybody and the more time that schools take to find out what each community group wants the better. If the whole community supports what is happening there are fewer opportunities for negative attitudes to develop. If the whole school has an effective ethos that promotes good, positive behaviour then classrooms will be peaceful learning environments.

Skills summary

This chapter has concentrated on the kinds of activities that need to be developed by the whole school as a way to improve teaching and learning. Some like the 3-metre rule or 'no put-downs' are relatively easy to implement at very little cost in both time and effort. But when we come to try to understand some of the barriers to learning and begin to link parents and families with the school's developments, there are long-term issues that may mean a radical shift in both school culture and how this relates to parents.

Activity 2.1

Moving away from retribution

If you want to consider a system of restorative justice and using pupils as mediators, you will have to move away from a system of control largely based on retribution (while keeping some of its strengths to deal with serious issues). Look at the statements below and try to work out how your school or department could move from left to right.

Behaviour problems are almost always seen as breaking rules, refusing to follow instructions etc.	Behaviour problems are related to damaging the well-being of an individual or group
Teachers focus on finding out who is guilty, who is to blame etc.	Teachers focus on finding out how those involved feel about what they have done and what they think needs to happen next
The wrongdoer(s) are in direct conflict with those in authority, i.e. teachers, who decide on any sanctions	There is dialogue and negotiation about how the problem can be solved via communication and cooperation
Any punishment is designed to be unpleasant and to deter and prevent similar behaviour in future	The goal is reconciliation (if the problem relates to conflict between pupils) or the pupil taking on board the idea of responsibility for his/her actions
The wrongdoing and sanction is impersonal and is largely perceived as being the individual or group against the school	Wrongdoing is seen as being between individuals and presents opportunities for learning
People (victims) affected by any wrongdoing or conflict between pupils are largely ignored and they can feel powerless in making any difference	All those involved are encouraged to try and think about the problem and how it can be resolved
The pupil who has misbehaved or caused a problem is only accountable in terms of receiving the appropriate sanction or punishment	The pupil is encouraged to think about being responsible for his/her actions and taking responsibility, about making the right choices and helping to put things right if they go wrong

Activity 2.2

A model for the whole school

Stage 1

The school's ethos needs to develop a sense of collective responsibility in all pupils so that they: <ul><li>have high self-esteem</li><li>mutually respect each other</li><li>know that there is a culture of acceptance and inclusion</li><li>empathise with each other in times of difficulty</li></ul>	All those who are part of the school, including support staff, governors and parents, need to accept and develop this ethos by using: <ul><li>essential rules</li><li>clear and consistent citizenship programmes</li><li>mentoring and mediating</li><li>negotiated essential rules and leisure time</li><li>the school council to address any issues</li></ul>

Stage 2

The ethos needs to demonstrate a positive approach to problem-solving and conflict resolution by adopting tactics such as: <ul><li>win–win strategies</li><li>negotiation skills</li><li>non-violent communication</li><li>empathy for others</li></ul>	The whole school (see above) will need: <ul><li>focused training</li><li>mediation training for pupils</li></ul>

Stage 3

Restorative approaches to conflicts and challenges will need: <ul><li>mediation skills</li><li>anger management skills</li></ul>	Appropriate members of the school community will need: <ul><li>further training</li><li>practice in the skills plus ongoing further training in mediation skills</li></ul>

Activity 2.3

Questionnaires for parents, pupils and teachers

Parents can respond to and ask the following question.

> Which of the following describes my child?
> - happy
> - safe
> - enjoying school
> - successful
> - well behaved
> - learning good behaviour
> - able to get on with other pupils
> - able to get on with adults in the school
> - being treated fairly by teachers and teaching assistants
> - being given the fullest opportunities to learn

Pupils often have other concerns and further questions that they would appreciate being asked.

> - Is there enough to do at break times?
> - If you don't understand something do teachers help you?
> - Is the work too hard?
> - Is the work too easy?
> - Is the school outside the classrooms safe?
> - Do teachers treat you fairly?
> - Are teachers strict enough?
> - Are all the adults fair?
> - Is there any bullying?

Teachers need to ask questions about the school/department.

> - Is the school environment pleasant to work in?
> - Is there a whole-school climate of positive behaviour management and discipline?
> - Are there enough resources to enable me to do my job?
> - Do I get support from other teachers and senior management?
> - Do I get support from parents?
> - Are decisions made after consultation?
> - Are my skills used effectively?
> - Am I trained effectively in any new skills that I might need?

3 Developing successful teaching

The first two chapters concentrate on whole-school supportive initiatives and developing an environment that makes effective teaching easier. But all the efforts of the school and of colleagues will not work if you do not use a whole range of skills and tactics to teach the curriculum and manage your classroom and teaching groups. Skilful teachers can make what they do look easy, but even experienced teachers in schools where there is a positive whole-school ethos can meet difficult and challenging classes and tutor groups. It helps if we all know what is successful and less successful about our teaching. Performance management together with classroom observations will help teachers to understand their areas of strength and those areas that need to be developed. Teachers also need to look at their own practice and make their own judgements about how effective they are on a more regular basis than that provided by an annual performance review.

When talking about primary schools, Pollard and Tann (1992) use the phrase 'reflective teaching' and suggest that this 'involves a willingness to engage in constant self-appraisal and development. Among other things it implies flexibility, rigorous analysis and social awareness' (p. 9). This applies equally to teachers in secondary schools.

Price (1992) suggests that teachers need to be aware of their own strengths and areas where they need to improve. He suggests a continuing self-audit or, as he describes it, 'self-appraisal':

> Self-appraisal is based on the job actually being done by each teacher in the context in which they are doing their job...No imaginary situations are involved. So participants can be provided with structured opportunities for reflecting on their work, such as prompt questions asking what aspects of the job are found most/least interesting, what helps/hindrances have been encountered in the job, what they were good/less good at etc. (p. 34)

Activity 3.1 (p. 62) is a useful method of self-audit that takes about 15 minutes to complete. In trying to recognise your strengths and weaknesses you begin to take the next step, which is to translate what you find into successful action.

Knowing yourself in this way is helpful because you are able to recognise what questions to ask yourself, what support you might need and what training and staff development will be helpful. Putting this another way, by evaluating yourself you can ascertain whether your teaching is as good as it could be, and if not, how it could be improved.

Important characteristics of how you teach

The self-audit in **Activity 3.1** (p. 62) focuses on practical issues such as planning, assessing, setting clear objectives and differentiating — in other words, what you should be doing. But to be successful in teaching you need to actually want to do the job well — and what is even more important is that you communicate this eagerness and this desire to your pupils. You need to show them that you want to teach them and that what *you* are teaching and *they* are learning is important. Some of the key characteristics are listed below. Ask yourself the following questions: Do I do this? If I don't, why not? If I did, would my teaching be more effective?

- **Be enthusiastic** — show that you are excited about teaching and your pupils might respond more energetically.
- **Be an expert** — always give the impression that you know everything. Do this by keeping up with new developments and using any professional development opportunities to maintain your expertise.
- **Organise your work and your time** — by being well organised, having structured routines and the ability to prioritise you will have more time to teach and relate to your pupils.
- **Work hard and energetically** — everyone appreciates hard work. You will be more admired if you get involved and are seen around the school talking and working with pupils both inside and outside the classroom.
- **Come to work in a good mood** — pupils do not need to be faced with your bad moods. You need to model good attitudes by teaching, listening and responding cheerfully.
- **Be a successful classroom manager** — you need to show that you are in control of your teaching space by having structures in place that reinforce all the appropriate and necessary rules.
- **Make sure that there is pace and progression in your teaching** — the speed that you teach the curriculum has to be related to pupil ability by being neither too fast nor too slow. The content also needs to progress so that repetition is kept to a minimum.
- **Work well with colleagues** — good teamwork is essential and you should be a willing group member who wants to be involved in delegation, change and decision-making.

- **Communicate well** — communication is a two-way progress, so you will need to read diaries and notice boards, and of course communicate effectively in lessons by setting clear, appropriate and easily understood objectives.
- **Question effectively** — asking both open-ended and closed questions is a powerful teaching tool because it encourages pupils to think.
- **Encourage successes** — it is important to make success accessible to both the academic and the non-academic pupil.
- **Have high expectations** — pupils should know that they are expected to do their best and that second-rate work, which is completed with little effort, is never acceptable.
- **Create a pleasant teaching space** — cheerful, bright and happy teaching spaces help to stimulate learning.
- **Build in flexibility** — lesson planning should be flexible enough so that if something really interesting turns up during a lesson you are able to give some time to it.

As well as having available most of the above characteristics there are four basic styles that can affect how you teach. **Activity 3.2** (p. 64) will help you to recognise what your dominant style is. If you are going to attempt to complete it, do so before you read the descriptions below, which begin to argue that some styles are more effective than others.

Authoritarian

This style places firm limits on all pupils. It is a teacher-dominated style, with pupils knowing that they must not interrupt and with few opportunities for discussion. As an authoritarian teacher you will prefer strict discipline and expect swift obedience. You will praise pupils for sticking to the rules and for following instructions. Part of an authoritarian style is for you to care very much that each pupil follows instructions and learns what they are supposed to be learning.

Authoritative

This style is sometimes known as the assertive style where teachers place limits and controls on their pupils but, at the same time, encourage a degree of independence. When you use this style you will offer explanations for rules and routines. If pupils are disruptive you are able to offer a polite but firm reprimand. After considering the circumstances, this can, and often is followed up by sanctions. As an authoritative teacher you will have a caring and nurturing attitude towards your pupils and offer a lot of praise and rewards. You will also encourage self-reliance and socially competent behaviour.

Laissez faire

This style places few demands or controls on pupils. You will accept pupils' impulses and actions and are less likely to monitor their behaviour. When it is necessary to control a pupil's behaviour, the kind of strategies that you use are likely to be inconsistent and you are more likely to be concerned with the pupils' emotional well-being than you are with classroom control. This means that it is difficult for pupils to learn what socially acceptable behaviour is. With few demands placed on them, pupils may have lower motivation and achieve less than they are capable of.

Indifferent

In this style, you will not be particularly involved in the classroom and you place few, if any, demands on your pupils, who may feel that you are not very interested in them. Lesson planning can be minimal and you will tend to use the same lessons every year without considering whether they work or not or whether the lessons will raise achievement in any way. Your classroom management and control may be poor and you may lack the skills, energy and motivation to improve it. The pupils quickly sense this indifferent attitude and, accordingly, little learning takes place. The majority of pupils will have low attainment and will lack self-control.

Teaching styles and classroom management

I hope that after analysing your dominant style you find that you are most effective when you are a combination of authoritarian and authoritative. If you are, it is more likely to mean that you have strategies in place that will help you solve the problem of how pupils learn effectively. In addition to this, Rogers (1991) suggests three different basic types of classroom discipline:

- **Preventative** — there has been careful planning in terms of rules, classroom organisation and the consequences of disruption.
- **Corrective** — where the teacher corrects disruptive behaviour in some way.
- **Supportive** — the corrective side of the process of discipline is supported by follow-up work so that supportive relationships are rebuilt and re-established.

Activity 3.3 (p. 65) is a list of classroom management skills (there are more below). When you have read each of the statements and ticked the appropriate boxes, look at the skills you use most often and also those you use least. Ask yourself:

- Are there some skills that you may as well forget about?
- Are there some you use a lot but just don't seem to work?
- Are there others that you don't use that might be more effective if you started using them more often?

If used consistently, many skills to help you deal with individual pupils and individual incidents can have a 'ripple effect'. This means that, when you are dealing with a specific problem caused by a particular pupil, the control tactic you use will be recognised and picked up by other pupils and have a positive effect on their behaviour and work rate as well. All control and class management tactics will work best if they are used within the following guidelines:

1 If you say you are going to take action, make sure you carry out the threat.
2 If you have to take action to prevent a certain kind of inappropriate behaviour, make sure that the action that you take is at the lowest possible level. Save your 'big guns' for really serious occasions.
3 Try to make sure that the classroom rules you establish cover most eventualities so that any action that you have to take will be pre-planned and you will have to make fewer ad hoc decisions.

Some pupils at certain ages will, of course, react differently to control tactics, and it may be the case that you will have to take decisions about using some of the following on their own or others linked together. As you read the tactics listed below, think about:

- When do I use this tactic?
- Does it work?
- If I don't use it, should I start using it?
- Which of the tactics will I never use?

Many of the strategies are worth practising, either on your own — in front of a mirror, perhaps — or if you are really brave, with a trusted friend. This may sound amusing and trivial but it isn't — it is very serious. For example, you need to learn how to look as assertive as possible when you frown. How authoritative do you really sound and look when you are calling someone's name? What do you need to do as you walk firmly towards a pupil?

Control tactics

Non-verbal control tactics:
- using eye contact
- raising the eyebrows during eye contact
- frowning
- giving a filthy look
- smiling
- using a calming gesture with your hands at the same time as smiling
- nodding at the same time as smiling
- using a quiet gesture of finger on lips on its own and with points 1 and 3

Sound as a control tactic:

- tapping on the desk with a hard object or closing the door loudly
- snapping fingers
- calling someone's name
- coughing
- using the same starting signal every time you are ready, such as 'Right. Everyone ready?' or 'I'm ready, let's start'

Contact as control tactic:

- sitting next to a pupil
- standing close to a pupil
- walking towards a pupil purposefully and silently with appropriate facial expressions
- walking towards a pupil saying his/her name and giving him/her specific instructions
- removing an object that is causing a problem such as a pencil, piece of paper etc.
- directing a pupil to another seat or out of the classroom

Classroom management

Good classroom management in the most effective classrooms is closely related to well-planned, interesting and carefully thought-out teaching that is closely matched to the needs and interests of the pupils. In fact, good teaching can be linked to the following seven aspects of classroom management. As you read the questions in each section, ask yourself the following:

- What aspects of these issues are you good at?
- What are you less good at and need to develop more?
- How are you going to improve in these areas?
- Who is available to help you?

1 The taught curriculum

- How broad, balanced, relevant and differentiated is the taught curriculum?
- Are your assessment and recording systems effective?
- Do you understand the content of the curriculum you are teaching?
- Are the outcomes you expect in your lessons interesting and varied?

2 Classroom organisation

- Does the physical layout of your classroom(s) create a positive learning environment?
- Are there enough appropriate resources for you to teach as effectively as possible?

- Do you use your resources well to benefit all pupils?
- Are your pupils grouped appropriately for the kind of teaching that you want to do?
- Are you able to use a teaching assistant to create smaller teaching groups?

3 Management of pupil activities

- If activities change in your classroom and pupils move from one activity to another, is this transition smooth with little disruption?
- Are you able to have 'eyes in the back of your head' and monitor all the activities going on in your classroom?
- Are you able to 'multitask'?

4 Classroom atmosphere or ethos

- Does the general classroom atmosphere promote good behaviour and positive relationships?
- Is there an atmosphere of productive interaction between teachers and pupils?

5 Routines

- Are the essential rules working or do they need to be changed?
- Are there enough formal routines in your classroom to contribute to a well-organised learning environment?
- Are the pupils clear about rules and routines?

6 Teaching strategies

- Do you state your lesson objectives clearly?
- Do you differentiate to meet the needs of all your pupils?
- Is your planning effective?
- Do you use a variety of teaching styles that promote clear learning responses?
- Have you the necessary skills to use if pupils are not responding appropriately?

7 Links between home and school

- How have you established links between home and school?
- Do you know the home backgrounds of the pupils in your class?
- Are there enough useful home–school links to help you take decisions about teaching and learning?
- What kind of communication between home and school do you use to help you understand your pupils better?

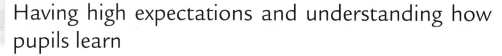

Having high expectations and understanding how pupils learn

It is a fact of life that bored pupils are difficult to teach. Planning lessons well and differentiating the work you set to meet the needs of different ability levels is essential. Each lesson you teach needs to cater for the learning needs of all pupils, from the gifted and talented to the less able. It is almost certain that your school, like every other school, will have an 'aims statement' that is similar to this:

> The school aims to provide a broad and balanced curriculum for all pupils...It values all its pupils equally...This relates to all pupils of all abilities and disabilities.

and/or:

> Our main aim is to enable every pupil to achieve his or her maximum potential.

One of the main problems when teaching mixed-ability groups is to provide work and activities that are challenging for every ability level. It is also important to be aware that different pupils will have different learning styles. For example, the different roles performed by different parts of the brain can have an impact on how we develop strategies for teaching them:

- The left side of the brain deals with logic, language, number, formulae, phonetics, reading systems and analysis. Pupils who use this side of their brain the most learn the details first and then move on to the whole picture.
- The right side of the brain gives an overview before moving to a study of the parts. It deals with patterns and forms, music, images and pictures, imagination, whole language reading and relationships.

What you actually do when you teach and what you ask pupils to do, usually favours the left side of the brain.

This is further complicated by the suggestion that pupils have three main types of learning style. Knowing what your pupils' learning styles are and being able to meet their needs is difficult, and even in the best classrooms some pupils will seem to be frustrated and not working to their full potential. However, if there is no match between how your pupils learn and how you are teaching, there may be some problems relating to motivation, achievement and standards.

You may be able to recognise some of your pupils in the descriptions of the three main learning styles below.

Visual learners

Visual learners (approximately 65% of children) take in new information through diagrams, the written word, charts and films. They will be less happy and less confident in lessons where they are not involved in note-taking and writing. To some extent, information does not exist for a visual learner unless it has been written down. They also follow you with their eyes, talk quickly and will tend to look into the distance when trying to work something out. They will use phrases such as: 'I see what you mean', 'Yes, that looks good, I can understand now', 'I get the picture', 'Yes, that looks right'. Reading is usually an activity that they prefer to do when relaxing.

Auditory learners

Auditory learners (approximately 30%) will prefer the spoken word and are usually very good listeners, although impatient to talk. Information that is written down will not be particularly meaningful until it has been heard. They will often tilt their heads to one side and sometimes repeat what has just been said in a sophisticated way. They are likely to say: 'That sounds good', 'I hear what you are saying', 'That rings a bell'. They will often talk to themselves or try to talk to other pupils and may not consider reading to be a very interesting activity.

Kinaesthetic learners

Kinaesthetic learners (around 5%) find it easier to learn by doing and getting physically involved. They will like to touch and get hold of things and will prefer to fidget and move around when doing any kind of work. They learn skills by imitation and practice. When they are working, they will look down at what they are doing rather than up at the teacher. They can appear slow to learn because the teaching styles used are less likely to suit their learning methods. They will say such things as: 'That feels right', 'That's a good idea', 'Let's do it this way'. When they are working in the classroom, they will talk to other pupils and will find it difficult to sit still.

There will be pupils using all three learning styles in your teaching groups and the challenge is to use teaching styles that meet the needs of them all. This is important because while all pupils will have one dominant style as well as a preference for another, their learning will be hindered if their dominant style is not catered for. You will probably already have recognised that most teachers, probably you included, are not geared to kinaesthetic learners. This will have a significant impact on individual pupils and affect their levels of achievement — and many more boys than girls fall into this category. The most important way forward is to adopt appropriate teaching styles.

Visual learners prefer to:
- write down key facts
- create pictures and diagrams
- use time lines and mind maps
- watch DVDs or films or presentations on computers or interactive whiteboards
- draw and graphically illustrate their work

Auditory learners prefer lessons where they:
- listen to presentations from teachers or peers
- read aloud to themselves
- make recordings of some kind or listen to recordings
- are allowed to verbally summarise key points in a lesson in their own words
- explain the lesson to someone else
- are allowed to sit for a period of time to think and internally verbalise what the lesson is about

Kinaesthetic learners learn more effectively if they:
- make models
- are physically involved in their learning by touching objects and using as much practical apparatus as possible
- use IT equipment in an interactive way
- record information immediately
- walk around the classroom occasionally
- underline and/or highlight key information
- make index cards or their own system of lists and memory aides

Meeting all these needs is daunting, but if we simplify it slightly it is possible in most lessons to utilise all three styles in the following ways:

1 Give the pupils opportunities to visualise the key messages by using pictures, videos/DVDs, ICT, interactive whiteboards etc.
2 Make sure that there is verbal input through talking, reading aloud, explaining information to each other.
3 Allow time for pupils to use practical activities, to move around the room and when using worksheets etc. to underline and highlight key information.

Getting this balance right is important. If you translate the percentages listed earlier into an average teaching group of, say, 30 children there will be 19 visual learners, 9 auditory and 2 kinaesthetic. The following figures show that the rate of knowledge retention varies from 5% if a pupil is being lectured to, to 90% if a pupil is able to teach another pupil what they have learned.

Style of teaching and learning	Average retention rates (%)
Lecturing	5
Reading	10
Audiovisual	20
Demonstration	30
Discussion	50
Practice by doing	75
Teach others	90

Skills summary

To summarise what are quite complex issues, the following list suggests ways in which you can be successful:

- Use any assessments of pupils' abilities and attainments as a starting point for teaching.
- Provide activities of sufficient variety and depth to allow for different levels of learning to take place.
- Differentiate by trying to use various starting points and tasks for different ability levels.
- Anticipate and expect different outcomes.
- Acknowledge that all pupils will need varying lengths of time to complete activities.
- Understand that each pupil will grasp new ideas in varying timescales.
- Group pupils in different ways for different tasks.
- Use a manageable number of differentiated teaching groups. No more than four is a manageable number.
- Plan realistic deadlines so that all pupils have a sense of achievement.
- Continuously assess teaching groups and give feedback about their learning and their successes.
- Use marking to inform pupils about their standard of achievement.

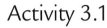

Activity 3.1

Self-audit

Read each of the following statements and tick the relevant box. Leave out any statements that do not apply to your school or your situation. When you have completed the self-audit, look carefully at those statements where you have ticked 'sometimes' and particularly 'never'. These are areas where you probably need to make improvements.

	Always	Sometimes	Never
Teaching in the classroom			
My planning is thorough and includes clear learning objectives			
I use teaching styles that are matched to the subject and pupils' learning styles			
I differentiate and set work that is matched to pupils' ability			
I use appropriate resources			
Homework is set that is linked to work in progress			
I mark all work so that it has a positive effect on pupil progress			
I set pupils tough individual targets			
Planning the curriculum			
I plan the curriculum I teach in the short and the medium term			
My planning meets the needs of pupils of all abilities			
My short-term planning allows for assessment opportunities in each lesson			
I enhance the curriculum by planning for visitors and for trips outside school			
Assessment recording and reporting			
I have procedures for monitoring the progress of each individual pupil			
Where appropriate I use assessment results, tests and examinations			
I keep full records of individual pupil performance			
I write accurate and helpful reports for parents			
I discuss progress with pupils on a regular basis			
Behaviour and attitudes			
I set high standards of behaviour in the classroom			

	Always	Sometimes	Never
The quality of relationships, in terms of politeness and friendships, that I expect in the classroom is high			
I have effective strategies for achieving good behaviour and good relationships			
My pupils respect one another			
My pupils respect their own and other pupils' property			
Pupils in my classes are encouraged to exercise responsibility			
Equal opportunities			
I organise my teaching groups to make provision for equality of opportunity			
The resources I use reflect the gender and ethnicity of the teaching group			
The outcomes I expect do not disadvantage any group of pupils			
Special educational needs (SEN)			
I use teaching assistants effectively to support SEN pupils			
I use external support effectively			
I am able to set appropriate objectives for SEN pupils			
I am able to use information in IEPs to set SEN targets and objectives			
I integrate pupils with SEN into all my teaching			
Teaching and whole-school issues			
I understand my curriculum and pastoral responsibilities			
I know what my performance management targets are and how I am going to meet them			
I know what is in my job description			
I have copies of and have read and understood all whole-school/department policies related to teaching, behaviour and health and safety			
Teaching and administrative organisation			
I always understand my own timetable			
I know what I have to do if I am ill and I cannot get to school			
I know who to contact for behaviour problems			
I understand what I have to do when pupils are absent or late			
I know where resources are and how to access them			

Activity 3.2

Classroom management style

Think back to some of your lessons during the last week, especially those that were very successful and those that were a lot less effective. Consider your classroom management style in these lessons. Then read the 12 statements, tick the appropriate box and add up your scores. Your highest scores will suggest your dominant classroom management style. If you have similar scores for two styles, this suggests that you are able to vary your style to fit different lessons and different circumstances.

Classroom management style	Strongly disagree (1 mark)	Disagree (2 marks)	Neutral (3 marks)	Agree (4 marks)	Strongly agree (5 marks)
1 If a pupil is disruptive I immediately punish him/her without any discussion					
2 I do not impose rules on my pupils					
3 I insist that my classroom is quiet so that my pupils can learn					
4 I am always concerned about what my pupils learn and how they learn it					
5 I do not consider late homework as my problem					
6 I do not like reprimanding pupils in case it hurts their feelings					
7 I do not consider lesson planning helps me teach well					
8 I always try to explain why there are certain rules					
9 I do not accept excuses for lateness					
10 I place greater emphasis on my pupils' emotional well-being than I do on classroom control					
11 When I am talking, my pupils know that they can interrupt if they want to ask a question					
12 I allow pupils to leave the room at any time in the lesson, if they need to					

Total for questions 1, 3 and 9   _____   =   Authoritarian style
Total for questions 4, 8 and 11   _____   =   Authoritative style
Total for questions 6, 10 and 12 _____   =   Laissez-faire style
Total for questions 2, 5 and 7   _____   =   Indifferent style

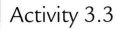

Activity 3.3

Effective classroom management skills

Read each of the following statements and tick the appropriate box.

An effective teacher can...	Not often	Often	Very often
organise and plan the curriculum to cater for pupils of different abilities			
ignore some kinds of disruptive behaviour			
give pupils choices that they are able to cope with			
find time to follow up behaviour problems and disruption later after the initial trauma has subsided			
build up a positive ethos in the classroom			
create an attractive and welcoming classroom environment			
recognise the importance of knowing what to say and how to say it when dealing with a pupil who is off-task and disruptive			
make available good, relevant and adequate resources			
create space for and know when to deal with pupils by removing them from friends and from the classroom			
use different kinds of questioning both to elicit information and to solve problems			
give simple, effective and formal warnings			
encourage pupils, often by praising and being enthusiastic about their achievements			
develop an ethos where respect for everyone is the norm			
plan the classroom in terms of seating, access to seats and equipment to avoid disruptive movement			
develop a work-orientated classroom with clear expectations about tasks and outcomes, i.e. what is expected at the end of a period of time			
use all kinds of techniques, including separating culprits from their peers and disciplining them on their own			
quickly re-establish a good relationship with a pupil who has been punished			
use other colleagues to help solve discipline problems			
remind pupils of stated and agreed classroom rules			
spot incidents coming and defuse situations			
work out long-term systems such as behaviour contracts and regular meetings with parents			

4 Classroom control

Controlling everything that happens in your classroom is essential. Without control there will be little effective teaching and you will have no control over what pupils learn; they will not achieve their full potential and standards will not rise.

One of the simplest starting points is to be able to demonstrate that you challenge and support pupils by:
- inspiring trust and confidence
- building learning commitment
- engaging and motivating them
- thinking analytically about what they need
- being able to take positive action to improve the quality of their learning
- using data and the evaluation of results to plan learning

Effective teacher behaviour

In order for effective teaching to take place, teachers have to be firm, fair and consistent. To maintain this consistency of approach you might also think carefully about developing the following four teaching and classroom management strategies:

1 **Praise** — this means that there is more praise than criticism. Some of this praise will be the kind of quiet encouragement that is part of any lesson and other praise will be public praise among classes, year groups and in full assemblies.
2 **Care** — all teachers need to show their pupils that they care both about their work and how they can reach even higher standards.
3 **Flexibility** — there will be times when you will find that teaching in a certain way just does not work. It is important that any attempts to standardise teaching methods and achieve a sense of a consistent approach does not totally inhibit creativity and that there is room for more flexible approaches when necessary.
4 **Perseverance** — this is really that old cliché: if at first you don't succeed try, try again. Despite the need for a consistent approach, there must be 'flexibility'. Perseverance can mean carrying on in a particular way to achieve success, but it can also mean trying something different to achieve the same ends.

Broad methods of control

Managing your classroom(s) to achieve control over what is happening is largely concerned with how the room is organised and what is actually taught as well as your own positive, appropriate and effective teaching techniques, many of which will be non-verbal, such as:

- having a confident upright stance
- moving purposefully round the room
- wearing smart clothes
- having a confident smile with direct, open eye contact
- making clear and direct eye contact with pupils you are talking to
- using appropriate gestures such as raised eyebrows, finger to lips, calming hand movements etc.

It is important to match your words to an appropriate non-verbal technique. For example, it is no good leaning on a radiator with a half smile, looking into the distance if you are in the middle of reprimanding a pupil for a bullying incident. Similarly, it is inappropriate to stand with hands on hips, glaring at a pupil, when you are praising his/her work.

Once you are equipped with such techniques it is possible to use the following broad approaches at different times, with different pupils and in different teaching groups:

- **Control by being in authority** — you will take most, if not all decisions and teach by telling rather than by explaining or justifying what you are doing. This kind of control is associated with strictness and formality, both in how you teach and how the classroom is arranged. It is possible to see authority and control of this kind as repressive and depriving pupils of exercising any choice, but if it is handled calmly and fairly it can produce a stable and predictable classroom atmosphere that many pupils from volatile and unpredictable home backgrounds can find beneficial.
- **Control by being permissive** — you will give fewer instructions, adopt a more flexible style and create an atmosphere that allows choice in which pupils are expected to take some responsibility for their own learning.
- **Control through successful relationships** — you will try to create a classroom atmosphere where learning will develop through good relationships between teacher and pupils and between pupils. You may have a policy where all pupils in your teaching group are asked their opinions, where a class council will flourish and where rules and working patterns may be partly negotiated.
- **Control by changing behaviour** — you will believe that good behaviour needs celebrating or reinforcing and that misbehaviour should, where possible, be ignored. There will be a system of positive rewards for good behaviour, and

those whose bad behaviour is ignored — where it is possible to ignore it — will be involved in behaviour contracts where their good and bad deeds are monitored by you or a teaching assistant on a daily or weekly basis.

- **Tactical control** — you will look for certain signs and react accordingly. For example, you will learn to spot the potential for misbehaviour before it happens and will be able to predict crisis points and move in to stop them before they escalate into more serious problems. If you use this method you will also be able to monitor the whole classroom all the time, which means that you are able to work with small groups and know what is happening in the rest of the room.

- **Control by knowing the class and the pupils** — you will know many of the details of the pupils who are in your teaching groups. This can involve understanding their social and financial conditions, religion, diet, beliefs etc. You will accept that sometimes external factors may impinge on what you are able to teach in the classroom as well as how pupils behave.

Beginnings

It is in your interest to make a positive impact when first meeting a class, returning after a holiday and even at the beginning of each day — and perhaps, if you want to make an impact several times a day, after every break and lunchtime. If you greet your class and/or tutor group cheerfully, openly and honestly at each meeting and give out signals that say, 'I am enjoying this, I like you and we are all going to work hard today,' it is bound to be more effective than if you begin each day tired and irritable showing little interest in the job or the pupils.

Montgomery (1989) suggests in a section headed 'Personal presentation in the classroom' (p. 19) that there are facial expressions that teachers use which can influence how the group or class reacts:

- The **'meeting of friends'** smile is an open-faced, direct gaze, with mouth slightly open showing upper teeth only and tilting at corners of mouth and eyes and crowsfeet wrinkles. The chin is tilted slightly upwards and small bags are produced under each eye by the lifting action of the face muscles. The eyebrows are quickly raised and dropped in recognition. This kind of first meeting smile tells everyone that you like them and they should feel significant.

- The **'not sure that I can cope'** smile is a fixed smile showing upper teeth, thin lower lip pulled in, upper teeth almost over lower lip as though biting, head down, eyes looking up slightly to the side, rather shyly. This smile signifies uncertainty, submission and anxiety to the onlooker and suggests a scared individual.

These descriptions may seem slightly strange and difficult to re-create, but they do emphasise that it is important to enter any teaching situation with a firm tread, head up, chin tilted slightly forward, shoulders back and an easy, confident pose. Montgomery is also simply emphasising the point that teachers need to look and behave as professionals by having a confident posture. Let's assume that your beginnings, your immediate starting points, last between 1 and 3 minutes. It is the time for settling everyone down, checking that everyone is in their place, resources are available and you are ready to start the introduction to the lesson.

In the few minutes that you have — and this can be at the beginning of the day, at the beginning of a new lesson or when you are starting after breaks and lunchtime — you will have to establish your position of authority with each teaching group by making several statements. These statements will have to be accompanied by appropriate body movements in order to be effective.

Why not try it? Read the example below. You could then complete **Activity 4.1** (p. 75) to remind yourself and illustrate what you do that is successful.

Opening statement
OK! Are you all ready? [name any individuals who are not paying attention] Right, let's make a start.
Body movement
Standing formally at the front, upright, slight smile, looking precisely round the room, especially at those who are obviously paying less attention, moving towards anyone who needs to be reminded personally.
What it should achieve
It should announce my presence and begin the quietening-down process ready to start the lesson straight away.

Before moving on to how to establish your own specific rules and relationships to help with classroom control, let's identify some more absolutely essential ways in which you will need to behave in order to establish control quickly at the beginning of lessons and activities and to maintain it throughout each and every day. **Activity 4.2** (p. 76) will help you to think about what you do as well as how you do it. It covers some familiar, as well as new strategies and suggests that teachers need to be firm, fair and consistent as well as being able to explain well.

Establishing working rules and relationships

All classes in whatever school have their rules and routines. They can be legislative rules relating to health and safety, whole-school rules emanating from the head teacher and senior managers, the agreed routines and essential rules established through meetings and consensus, and routines that you have established in your classroom in order to create the kinds of behaviour and relationships that you want when you are teaching.

Some of these rules are essential. They will be written down and will have been created through discussion and negotiation — perhaps through the use of a class and/or school council. At the same time, you will have to create instant and specific codes of behaviour throughout the day that are part of the general and essential rules but serve as constant reminders. Specific examples might include:

- Don't lean back on your chair it is dangerous.
- Put your chair under the table before you leave the room.
- Don't forget to put your hand up every time you answer a question.

Whatever specific rules you have in your classroom, they have to be meaningful to the pupils as well as necessary for high-quality teaching and learning to take place. At the same time, there has to be a distinction between rules and routines that create and preserve a harmonious working atmosphere and those that are sanctions and punishments.

The Elton Report (1989) has some important things to say about this distinction: 'Our evidence suggests that schools which put too much faith in punishments to deter bad behaviour are likely to be disappointed.' Mortimore et al. (1988) found that behaviour tended to be worse in junior schools (and I see no reason why this shouldn't apply to secondary schools) which emphasised punishments rather than rewards: '...the more punishments listed, the more negative the effect seemed to be' and '...punitive regimes seem to be associated with worse rather than better standards of behaviour. This does not mean that punishments are not necessary... The message seems to be that, in order to create a positive atmosphere, *schools need to establish a healthy balance between punishments and rewards*' (pp. 98–99) (my italics).

It also seems to be the case that some rules are more important than others. **Activity 4.3** (p. 77) is a comprehensive list of different kinds of rules. They include those relating to:

- relationships
- classroom space
- equipment and resources
- work
- noise and talking
- movement and safety

Some of the rules will be inappropriate for your particular pupils. Once you have established the minimum number of rules that you need in your classroom, you need to explain them to your pupils. This is not a beginning of the year or beginning of the term event. Like all of us, pupils have both short and selective memories and because of this you will have to explain and go over rules sometimes on a daily and weekly basis or each time you meet a particular group of pupils. How this is done effectively will depend on how you approach discipline, the whole-school ethos, how your pupils normally behave and their age and ability.

Here are some examples of how rules actually work:

- **Laying down the law** — (point to a particular group of pupils or to an individual) 'Stand up and come here. You do not work making that amount of noise. Now go back and work properly and quietly.'
- **Giving an explanation** — 'You must put up your chairs to help the cleaner when he/she sweeps the classroom floor.'
- **Expressing righteous indignation** — 'I am really disappointed in you. Never do that with your pencil/compasses/pen etc. You might hurt someone.'
- **Generalising** — 'I'd like to see a few more good manners today please.'
- **Being calmly specific** — 'Helen, no one is allowed to shout out. You must put your hand up.'
- **Asking general questions** — 'Why is it important to be careful when you are using some of the technology equipment?'
- **Negotiating rules** — 'When you are doing design technology there are far too many of you moving round the room. How can we stop that happening next week?'
- **Asking specific questions** — 'Why do I tell you not to push when you come into the classroom?'

Rewarding pupils

The quotations from Elton and Mortimore et al. suggest that behaviour management based only on punishments are counterproductive. Most schools will have a negotiated system of rewards using stickers, charts, certificates and public recognition of success. A programme that involves essential rules, leisure time and rewards works well because there is a balance between rewards and sanctions. What we are aiming for when we give rewards is to reinforce exactly what we want in terms of pupil behaviour and learning. For this to be effective, you will be good at both knowing what you want and inspiring pupils to want the same thing by reinforcing the right behaviour and attitudes. You can do this by offering two basic kinds of rewards:

1 **External rewards** — these are given to pupils and have been earned. They are often visible, like a sticker or certificate or a comment in a report or home–school book. External rewards often mean public recognition either in the classroom or in assemblies.

2 **Internal rewards** — these usually come from within and are feelings of satisfaction when something has been done well. Praise, a smile, a word of encouragement from an adult can often trigger off a person's internal rewards system.

It is important to have a balance of rewards that works. These may include 'verbal', 'symbolic' or 'tangible' rewards such as:

- **Praise and other verbal reinforcement** for such things as correct answers, accurate work, improved test scores, behaving appropriately, higher achievement.
- **Symbolic rewards** — such as gold stars, name on noticeboards or charts.
- **Token rewards** — such as points, marks or tokens, which are valueless in themselves but which can be collected and added up to give a reward that is tangible, can be seen or is an activity or public praise at a rewards ceremony.
- **Tangible rewards** — these can be gifts, prizes or certificates, cups, badges etc. They are usually presented in public in such places as assemblies.
- **Activity rewards** — these include free time or activities arranged through leisure time, extra time during breaks and being allowed to go on an outside visit.

It is important that any kind of praise or reward is earned. Pupils will usually despise arbitrary rewards given out for activities or behaviour that they can achieve easily. Such a reward system will not change behaviour or raise standards in any way. In fact, pupils who are rewarded for just doing what they know they can do easily will often achieve less than those who are not rewarded at all.

Effective rewards and praise:
- specify exactly what the reward is for
- recognise precisely what the pupil has achieved or accomplished
- provide clear information to pupils about what they have achieved
- are given in recognition of real effort or success at difficult (for the specific pupil) tasks
- link success to pupils' efforts and imply that similar successes are expected in future
- focus the pupils' attention on their own achievements

Ineffective rewards and praise:
- are delivered randomly or unsystematically
- don't require much effort on the part of pupils
- often reward participation in the lesson or task rather than real achievement
- provide no information to pupils about their ability, effort or success
- are given without any regard to the effort expended or the meaning of the accomplishment to the pupil

Activity 4.4 (p. 79) gives five realistic situations that could occur in one of your teaching groups or in your school. They could be useful for you to consider in the context of your own and your school's praise and reward system.

Setting behaviour targets

This section suggests several ways in which pupils can be persuaded to take some charge of their own behaviour and contains a number of examples of reports and contracts that can be used with individual pupils. Using any of these strategies, however, takes time and your school or department may have shorter and more appropriate strategies for you to use. The reports and contracts are certainly not for routine types of behaviour that happen at some time in all classrooms. They should only be used when other tactics have failed, or as part of a series of techniques when a pupil's behaviour is difficult and long term.

The *Personal disruption identification form* (see **Activity 4.5**, p. 80) is intended for use with an individual pupil. Its success depends on a meeting with the pupil, and parents recognising that the pupil's behaviour is unacceptable. It is, in essence, a collaboration between pupil, teacher and parent. If this happens, then the form can be a useful way for the pupil to both accept that there is a problem and to start doing something that will help solve it.

The *Behaviour monitoring form* (**Activity 4.5**, p. 81) is for the pupil to use daily to monitor his/her behaviour and for the teacher to use as a tool for discussing what it is that the pupil is doing. Be warned that this is time consuming. It requires all of the pupil's teachers for a given day to monitor what he/she is doing approximately every hour. Everyone involved must be able and willing to carry on using the form. It is also no good just giving the form to the pupil — you will need to read through the instructions first with him/her. It would be useful to give examples of good and bad behaviour so that he/she has some idea about what to write in the 'How I behaved' column. In addition, make it clear that if a teacher sees him/her doing something unacceptable then they will tell the pupil to write it down. The teacher comments should be kept brief and to the point. It is also important to offer the carrot-and-stick principle to a pupil who has to be on this kind of behaviour programme. For example, four good comments a day means a very small reward; three days in a row with four good comments each day means a better reward etc. Conversely, four bad comments a day means a small sanction; three days each with four bad comments means a larger sanction etc. However, if this happens, I would suggest that the exercise is having no impact and should be stopped.

Another form that is worth trying is the more formal *Pupil/teacher/parent contract* (**Activity 4.5**, p. 82). It involves preparation and discussion with all three parties. When such meetings are set up, it is important that the bad behaviour that is to be discussed and modified has been clearly identified. The teacher must take the lead in deciding how behaviour should be modified, although it is useful and diplomatic to allow some negotiation with the pupil and parent. During the discussion it is important to complete the section on the form headed 'Good behaviour that will replace the bad behaviour'. This will give you an opportunity to restate what is and is not acceptable behaviour. What you suggest for this section needs to be in the form of small but precise and achievable steps, e.g. 'I will stay sitting down for at least 5 minutes at a time' or 'I will always put my hand up instead of shouting out answers'. The 'daily comments' should be completed for at least 5 days before the contract is reviewed with the pupil. Involve the parents again if you feel that it is useful and don't forget to feed back to pupil and parents both positive and negative views. If the pupil has done well, tell him/her; if he/she hasn't, also tell him/her and complete the form for a second week.

Skills summary

This chapter suggests some useful strategies that have recognised the importance of:

- beginnings of lessons
- the content of the curriculum
- planning and preparation of lessons
- transitions between activities
- rules, rewards and sanctions
- teacher's attitude, manner and confidence

Activity 4.6 (p. 83) is a questionnaire and covers many of the strategies that have been discussed.

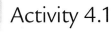

Activity 4.1

Beginning a lesson

Write down and remind yourself of the successful techniques that you use to start lessons.

Opening statement
Body movement
What it should achieve

Activity 4.2

Control tactics

Read each statement and write down what you do that is successful. If there are areas that you find difficult to complete, it might be worth thinking what you might be able to do in these circumstances that would make you even more effective.

Firm — by controlling pupils without being too punitive

How do you do it?

Fair — by consistently being perceived as fair, in the sense that only the wrongdoers get punished and there are never any blanket punishments

How do you do it?

Consistent — by creating a well-organised atmosphere with plenty of recognised praise

How do you do it?

Explaining well — so that pupils know exactly what they have to do, how work is to be completed and what they need to achieve to make progress

How do you do it?

Respectful — by treating all pupils equally and allowing them to retain their dignity

How do you do it?

Friendly — by being amicable without being over-familiar

How do you do it?

Supportive — by helping pupils to achieve good results and praising them for their efforts

How do you do it?

Activity 4.3

Important and less important rules

Read the following list of rules, which can be used to put together your classroom essential rules. Against each one write down one of the following scores:

1 = this rule is vitally important
2 = this rule is reasonably important
3 = this rule is not really important
4 = this rule is of no importance whatsoever

Rules relating to relationships

Be considerate to other people	
Share and cooperate	
Be thoughtful and polite	
Be well mannered	
Don't ever hit anyone else	
Don't ever verbally abuse anyone else	
Don't ever ridicule anyone else	

Rules relating to classroom space

Don't go into classrooms at break or during lunchtimes without permission	
Always use classrooms for work and not play	
Don't touch anyone's work when you move from your seat	
Always walk and never run in the classroom	

Rules relating to equipment and resources

Put things away when you have used them	
Keep all your books and equipment tidy	
If you have made a mess make sure that you clear it up	
Put everything away at the end of each lesson	
Respect other people's property	
Don't write on desks or books	
If you borrow something return it	

Rules relating to work

Hand in your homework on time	
Make sure your work is always as neat as possible	
Work on your own quietly and peacefully	
If you are asked to work in a group, do so in an appropriate way	
Never interfere with or distract other people who are working	
Work quietly if the teacher has to leave the room	

Rules relating to noise and talking

Don't talk when the teacher is talking to the class	
If you are working in a group only talk about the work that has been set	
Don't talk or interrupt if another pupil is talking to the class	
Never shout out	
Always put your hand up if you want to answer a question	
Be absolutely silent when registers are being taken	

Rules relating to movement and safety

Don't run, push or shove in the classroom	
Take care with equipment that might be hazardous	
Ask if you want to leave the room	
Don't wander around the room and move from seat to seat	
Don't swing on your chair or move anyone else's chair	

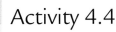
Activity 4.4

Praise and reward scenarios

Read each of the situations and consider the following:

- What reward would you give in this situation?
- Why would you give a reward and what would it achieve?
- How would you give a reward in this situation, e.g. quietly without anyone knowing other than the pupil receiving the reward; publicly in the classroom; publicly in an assembly?

Situation 1

A pupil not renowned for her neatness has just produced a carefully presented piece of writing.

Situation 2

A rather disruptive boy who finds it difficult not to talk and distract both himself and other pupils completes a piece of work at the same time as everyone else.

Situation 3

A pupil who you told off earlier for shouting out answers to questions has just put her hand up twice and given the correct answers.

Situation 4

One of the pupils in your tutor group has just won a painting competition out of school, organised by a local supermarket.

Situation 5

During a test, half of the pupils in one of your classes scored really well.

Activity 4.5

Personal disruption identification form

Name .... **Class** ....
Date form completed..
What I did (describe what you did in your own words):
What school/tutor group/essential rule I broke:
Why I did it (describe this in your own words):
What I should do to stop myself from doing it again:
Who do I need to apologise to?
Teacher's comments:
Parent's comments:
What follow-up is needed:
Signed (pupil) ....
Signed (teacher) ....
Signed (parent)..

Behaviour monitoring form

Instructions

This form is divided into five spaces — one for each hour you are in lessons today. Think how you are behaving and every time you know you are doing well, write it down. Do the same if you are behaving badly. Write VG for very good, G for good, B for bad, and VB for very bad. You decide what to write unless a teacher tells you to write something.

At the end of every hour, take the form to your current teacher and he/she will add a comment. At the end of each day, you must talk to your form tutor before you go home.

Name .... **Class**		
Date form completed..		
How I behaved	**Mark**	**Teacher comment**

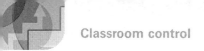

Pupil/teacher/parent contract

Pupil's name .... **Teacher's name** ....

Date started.. **Class** ....

Bad behaviour that needs changing:

Good behaviour that will replace the bad behaviour:

Teacher help that is needed:

Parent help that is needed:

Daily comments:
Day 1

Day 2

Day 3

Day 4

Day 5

Signed (pupil) ....

Signed (teacher) ....

Signed (parent)...

Activity 4.6

Behaviour management strategies

Read each of the statements and decide whether you are effective (E) or ineffective (I). Circle the appropriate letter E or I.

Use the space in the following ways:
- If you are effective (E), write briefly what you do that makes you effective.
- If you think you are ineffective (I), suggest what you need to do to improve, the kinds of training needs you have and who in your school might be able to help.

Lesson beginnings

I start each lesson positively with a clear signal	E	I
All pupils are encouraged to start each lesson promptly	E	I
All pupils know exactly what to do at the beginning of my lessons	E	I

Content of the lessons

The work I set is differentiated for all ability levels	E	I
I am able to set work that matches individual needs	E	I
The work I set is interesting and grabs the pupils' attention	E	I
The work I set is never too easy or too hard	E	I

Planning and preparation of lessons

I always set clear learning objectives and tell pupils what they are	E	I
My lesson planning is part of a medium and long-term plan	E	I
I always know what I am doing at each stage of the lesson	E	I
If I need different resources, such as videos/DVDs, IT access and OHTs, I don't leave this until the last minute	E	I
There are always assessment opportunities within my lessons	E	I

Transitions between activities

I make sure that transitions between different activities are smooth and trouble free	E	I
I make sure that there are no opportunities for excessive noise or movement between activities	E	I
I plan transitions — they don't just happen	E	I

Rules, rewards and sanctions

There is a list of basic classroom rules (essential rules)	E	I
I make it clear to all pupils what the rewards are	E	I
I make it clear what the sanctions are	E	I
I am always fair and consistent in applying the rules, the rewards and the sanctions	E	I

Teacher's attitude, manner and confidence

I dress appropriately and am confident and assertive in the classroom	E	I
I am approachable in lessons and model the kind of behaviour I expect	E	I
I am able to smile, frown and use all the appropriate and necessary body language	E	I

5 Teacher–pupil relationships

It seems reasonable to assume that the better and more positive the relationships between you and your pupils, the easier it will be to work alongside each other in a creative and supportive way. We must avoid situations where pupils feel that relationships are negative, and avoid creating a culture where they are unable to reach their full potential because they are afraid of making mistakes and are not encouraged to try and to persevere.

There are basically two teacher types who develop relationships resulting in a particular classroom 'atmosphere', 'ethos' or 'culture'. As a **provocative** teacher you will, because of how you behave, provoke difficult relationships and will usually try to create a narrow, teacher-guided environment where there is little tolerance for the individual and where punishment rather than praise is the norm. If you work in this way there will be lots of opportunities for on-task working, but because of the nature of your relationships off-task behaviour will be preferred by many of the pupils. You may have high expectations but outcomes will be lower and often of a predictable sameness. On the other hand, as a **supportive** teacher you will behave in such a way that you are able to work closely with your pupils who will be given an opportunity to grow and develop in a variety of ways and will be encouraged to produce a variety of outcomes. You will create an atmosphere that is firm, fair and consistent but also tolerant, with high expectations and a high proportion of on-task working.

As a **provocative** teacher you may:
- assume that pupils don't want to work and, when they don't work, there is a kind of self-fulfilling prophecy that it is impossible to provide the right conditions in which pupils will work
- believe that discipline is a confrontation that has to be won
- be unable to defuse situations
- frequently issue unreal ultimatums that lead to more confrontations
- use inconsistent punishments
- give preferential treatment to some pupils and not to others
- always expect certain pupils to behave badly
- make negative comments about pupils in public

As a **supportive** teacher you will usually:

- assume that everyone wants to work and, if they don't, the planning, resources, classroom conditions etc. are at fault rather than the pupils
- avoid any kind of favouritism
- avoid confrontation
- never make any negative comments about pupils in public
- give pupils the space to back down and save face if they have been badly behaved
- assume that pupils will behave well
- be firm and fair when it comes to both rewards and sanctions
- care about and trust pupils

The questionnaire in **Activity 5.1** (p. 99) is a useful starting point for examining the kinds of behaviour that you use to develop effective relationships within your teaching groups. After you have completed it you need to think about the kinds of responses that you have made. The assumption is that most, if not all of the responses will be 'often' (O) or 'sometimes' (S), with the majority of responses being (O). If you answered 'never' (N) to the majority of the questions, perhaps it is worth asking about the quality of the relationships in your classrooms and with your teaching groups. It is also worth thinking about the kinds of actions suggested by the questionnaire and how they will affect relationships and, subsequently, the kinds of teaching and learning that will be successful.

After you have completed the questionnaire, there are other questions that you can ask yourself that relate to what it means to be a supportive teacher:

1 What would happen and what kinds of relationships would you have if you didn't listen when the pupils in your classes were talking to you?
2 What would happen if you didn't try to extend and motivate all your pupils?
3 What would happen if you didn't see the occasional behaviour problem as a routine part of teaching but saw each one as a personal insult?
4 What would happen to the quality of relationships in your lessons if you constantly used humiliation as a basic control technique?
5 What would the quality of relationships be like if the pupils in your class could tell that you hated teaching them and were miserable all the time?
6 What would the pupils feel like if blanket punishments were used more frequently than praise?

Establishing good relationships

The almost forgotten, underused and neglected report, *Discipline in Schools: Report of the Committee of Enquiry Chaired by Lord Elton* (known as the Elton Report) takes the idea of positive relationships a step further by relating it to concepts such as 'popularity' and 'classroom climate'. Teachers who can achieve these good relationships are described in the following ways (the italics are mine):

> [They] create a classroom climate in which pupils lose rather than gain popularity with their classmates by causing trouble. They can also spot a disruptive incident in the making, choose an appropriate tactic to deal with it and nip it in the bud. In their relationships with their pupils they always seem to know what is going on behind their backs. Good group managers understand how groups of young people relate to each other and to teachers. They also understand and are in full control of their own behaviour. They model the good behaviour they expect from pupils. *All this requires an impressive range of skills* (pp. 67–68)

Building up and sustaining relationships is difficult, but it should be part of your repertoire of skills, strategies and styles. The list in **Activity 5.2** (p. 100) both complements and extends the statements and questions in the *Relationships questionnaire* (**Activity 5.1**). As you read each one, ask yourself:

- Why having this skill will make it easier to establish positive relationships.
- Why it will be difficult to establish positive relationships if you don't have this skill.

Let's now synthesise the assumptions that have been made so far in this chapter, and especially in your responses to the two questionnaires, by reducing them to five basic principles which, if used consistently, should help create a positive atmosphere and better teacher–pupil relationships:

1 **Let your pupils know that you value them** — all of us need to see ourselves as able to succeed. Pupils need to be treated with respect, valued as individuals and encouraged to work to their potential.

2 **Teach relevant lessons** — you are able to interpret the content of the curriculum into interesting and relevant experiences for your pupils. This will mean that it is important that you know your pupils, their interests, their strengths and their weaknesses. By talking to them, you will know what activities are likely to stimulate them and how you can help them to learn.

3 **Help your pupils to achieve success** — if pupils experience success, they are more likely to want to repeat the activity, or one that is similar. It is important to differentiate and provide work that is suitable and challenging for all abilities.

4 **Set appropriate objectives** — when you plan your lessons you need to set clear and easily understood objectives. If you are not clear what is to be achieved then the pupils won't be either. Setting clear objectives also makes it clear to your pupils what you will be assessing.

5 **Plan the organisation of your classroom** — the way in which your classroom is organised in terms of furniture, seating arrangements etc. is an important part of your classroom management strategy. Whole-class teaching, teaching

groups and individuals are all important and need to take place. Pupils need to have their own space for working.

Assertive teaching

In an earlier chapter, Montgomery's (1989) idea of 'personal presentation' in the classroom was mentioned. She argued that for teachers to be effective they need to have a personal presence — a kind of charisma — and one of the most successful ways of doing this is to be **assertive**. In many ways, assertion is about using the force of your personality to build up and develop the kinds of relationships that you want, rather than what your pupils or even other colleagues might want. Assertion is also about 'you' and your rights and is achieved without having to be either **aggressive**, or **passive**. In fact, if you are an aggressive person you are likely to become angry easily and may be volatile, often verbally insulting and even violent. If you adopt too passive a role you will usually be meek, put upon and so mild-mannered that colleagues and pupils are able to persuade you to do things and behave in ways that are negative and counterproductive.

Activity 5.3 (p. 101) is a grid of words that may be thought of as either 'assertive', 'passive' or 'aggressive'. It would be worth completing before you read any further.

You should have placed 'AS' for assertion alongside the following words: confident, knowledgeable, firm, fair, in control and thoughtful. It might be useful to think about how behaving assertively will improve your teaching ability and your all-round class-room skills and relationships. At the same time you might also consider avoiding aggression by not getting: angry, volatile, hot tempered or out of control. Equally, passivity and the kinds of behaviour associated with it, which include being put upon, lacking in confidence, timid, mild, meek and complacent, are more likely to lead to the kinds of relationships in your lessons that will inhibit high-quality teaching.

Assertiveness is all about being responsible for your own behaviour by respecting others and being honest. An assertive person is able to say what they want and feel, but not at the expense of other people. It is also about being self-confident and positive and having the ability to handle conflict by reaching acceptable compromises.

Aggression means trying to get your own way by making other people feel useless, worthless or small. It doesn't always have to involve conflict, but it usually does either by causing verbal or even physical hostility.

Passivity means ignoring your own interests and allowing others to manipulate you. It often means denying your own feelings by not being active and pro-active and not recognising that you have needs and goals.

A good relationship with colleagues and pupils is not a one-way process and you, as well as pupils, for example, must have rights. Think of these rights as applying to you and your pupils and consider how they will help develop positive relationships:

- I have the right to be taken seriously.
- I have the right to set class priorities.
- I have the right to express feelings and opinions.
- I have the right to say 'no'.
- I have the right to make mistakes at times when I am trying my best.
- I have the right to be in control of my own classroom/teaching space.

It is possible to learn how to be assertive. This can apply when you are dealing with pupils, colleagues and parents. By being assertive in difficult circumstances, it is possible to improve your feelings about yourself, give yourself confidence and prevent yourself from feeling powerless and out of control.

Step-by-step guide to assertion

This example (related to pupils) gives an outline of what to do when you need to be assertive. It starts with a simple scenario:

> You have had to speak firmly to a pupil who has been calling other pupils names that they have found distressing. As you are speaking to him/her, he/she starts shouting that he/she hates you and that everyone is always picking on him/her.

Now read the step-by-step guide to assertion below. As you read it, try and change it to your own words to reflect what you would actually say for each of the steps. A blank step-by-step guide is included as **Activity 5.4** (p. 102) so that you can practise by creating your own scenario and your own script, which can be specific to your needs, your pupils, your teaching groups or even colleagues or difficult parents. It is possible to practise being assertive and get better at it. There are further details in Smith (2000).

> **1 SUMMARISE** the behaviour that created the problem simply, unemotionally and straightforwardly.
>
> e.g. 'I don't like it when you call other people names and I certainly will not allow anyone to shout at me.'

> **2 STATE** exactly how you feel, not how anyone else feels.
>
> e.g. 'I am very concerned that you have been name calling and I am sad, upset and angry that you feel you have to shout at me in that bad tempered way.'

3 **DESCRIBE** clearly and simply why you feel like this.

e.g. 'First of all you know what the essential rules are and I feel concerned because name calling is cruel and unfriendly. Shouting at me makes me feel extremely unhappy because you know that this is not allowed and it is seriously breaking the rules.'

4 **SYMPATHISE or EMPATHISE** with the pupil's point of view.

e.g. 'I can understand that some of the other pupils irritate you and I am sure that I make you cross sometimes.'

5 **SPECIFY** exactly what you would like the pupil to do. You must also say what you would be willing to do to find a solution, a compromise or a way out of the current situation.

e.g. 'I want you to stop shouting instantly and I want you to promise me that you will stop calling other pupils names. If you have got a problem with some of your friends, you must tell me and I will try and help you.'

6 **DECIDE** what your response will be. It is important that whatever you decide should clarify your position without threatening the pupil.

e.g. 'If you calm down immediately you will be able to stay doing the same work as everyone else and I will talk to you later when you are calmer.'

Assertive body language and repeat, repeat, repeat

Being assertive has to be matched with the appropriate body language which includes:

- walking into the classroom upright, tall, dignified and smartly dressed
- standing straight, head held high, balanced on both feet
- moving round the room purposefully, knowing where to stand, when to stand and when to sit
- using a firm, clear and steady authoritative and sincere voice
- using fluent and unhesitating speech, which tells pupils that you are in charge and that it is important to listen
- maintaining eye contact without appearing to be staring
- having an open and friendly smile together with other appropriate facial expressions such as frowning, disapproval etc.

Another assertion technique, which can be used in most situations where there has been inappropriate behaviour, is repetition. This entails repeating the message that you are trying to get across. This technique is especially useful in situations where there is conflict and where you are telling someone something, correcting him/her or expressing an opinion that the pupil is trying either to deny or not to hear.

It usually works as a strategy because pupils find it uncomfortable to listen to repetition for too long. Many challenging pupils are masters at the art of sidetracking and introducing irrelevant information. Stay calm and, using the appropriate body language, keep repeating the point you want to make.

Here is an example of repetition. You, the teacher (T) are telling a pupil (P) not to run in the corridor. The pupil is agitated and denying it although you saw it happen.

> T: I don't want to see you running in the corridor again.
>
> P: It wasn't me, I was walking.
>
> T: You were not walking, you were running and I do not want to see you doing it again.
>
> P: There were lots of other people doing it.
>
> T: That's not the point. The point is that you were running in the corridor and you must not do it again.
>
> P: I was in a hurry to get to the classroom.
>
> T: Let me say it again, I don't ever want to see you running in the corridor again...

Relationships and specific teaching styles

How you manage pupils in the classroom will be the main starting point for both effective relationships and positive attitudes. Your behaviour will influence your pupils and create an atmosphere where effective learning will flourish. There are seven aspects of your behaviour which seem to have the most influence:

1 **Teacher attitude** — this should be firm, fair and consistent.
2 **Teachers supporting pupils** — how you work alongside pupils of all levels of ability but especially those who are off-task and, perhaps, misbehaving.
3 **Spoken behaviour** — how you use your voice for different purposes.
4 **Non-verbal behaviour** — how you use your body as part of your repertoire of skills.
5 **Eye contact** — how you look at pupils when you are rewarding them or imposing sanctions.
6 **Teacher reactions** — your responses to disruption and conflict are about remaining calm, not getting aggressive, and minimising the amount of time that disruptions are allowed to interrupt teaching and learning.
7 **Control style** — this includes the techniques and strategies that are used to manage behaviour within the context of the classroom.

You may recognise some of these aspects of teacher behaviour because, apart from 'control styles' which will be examined later, they are, in many ways, summarising several of the previous sections.

Activity 5.5 (p. 103) looks at three different groups of teacher behaviour that you may use or want to start using. It should be completed before you read the explanations below. As you read the definitions of each style, try to place them in context by thinking about your own situation and ask yourself what effect using this style will have on relationships and learning with your teaching groups.

- **Authoritarian** — if you behave in this way you will see power over pupils as an end in itself and, in order to gain and sustain this power, may use embarrassment and humiliation as a technique. It is a defensive 'us' and 'them' situation where you will want to win at all costs. As an authoritarian teacher, for example, you will dislike the use of cooperative discussion groups and you may be capable of being hostile, rude and aggressive. Rather than reflect on your own practice you will always blame the pupils, resources, colleagues etc.
- **Decisive** — rather than just stating the rules, as a decisive teacher you will negotiate and develop them with your pupils. Within a few days of meeting a class, you will develop strategies for handling misbehaviour and encouraging effective learning. You will recognise the inevitability of certain kinds of minor disruption and adopt the necessary techniques. Cooperation is encouraged by not creating an 'us' and 'them' situation. You will also be good at humour, repartee and general pupil–teacher conversation. You will show your pupils that you like them and, rather than nag, will be calm and always assertive.
- **Indecisive** — you will be conscientious and know what to do in the classroom, but not necessarily how to do it. You will want to be liked and yet not know how to go about achieving this state. While not wanting to show anger and bad temper, you will not know how to assert your rights and will allow pupils to dominate the classroom and create their own agenda. Rather than issue direct statements and commands, you will often enter into fruitless dialogues with pupils who are disruptive and sometimes lose your temper and then feel guilty.

Techniques for behaviour management

Imagine this scenario: you have planned a brilliant lesson on an important and interesting subject that your pupils need to learn about and you have differentiated the work well. If this is typical of how you work and how conscientious you are, then the last thing you want is off-task behaviour and inappropriate activities by the pupils. Teaching techniques to prevent this happening don't have to be complicated. One of the simplest and most useful strategies is to be aware of where you are in the classroom and how you move around.

It is important to use eye contact to express emotions and feelings and also to use your eyes to sweep the room quickly and take in most, if not everything, that is happening. This might appear to be common sense but it is well worth considering in more detail. There are areas of the classroom that you can't see if you stay in the same place, which is why it is important to move about constantly and place yourself in different parts of the room.

In previous sections classroom control has been mentioned alongside such phrases as 'managing inappropriate behaviour'. Some of the techniques, however, have been examined in isolation. For them to be most useful and effective, they need to be put together as a sequence of actions. Wragg (1984) makes it clear that 'control' of both pupils and the curriculum is one of the most important skills for teachers, and the key to effective teaching and learning. Smith (1996) suggests that as well as reading about similar control techniques as a series of actions, '...try practising in the mirror. If you have a sympathetic family or a trusted colleague, try performing each control sequence in front of them. Remember the cliché: "practice makes perfect"? Well it works!' (p. 15)

Read each of the control sequence examples below. Then try and present your own script of what you would do.

Control sequence 1

This is a good starting point when pupils are behaving inappropriately:

- **Signal of action** will be one of your usual signals such as a cough, look or glare.
- **Move close** is the follow-up to the signal of action and it usually takes place at the same time as the signal of action.
- **Take action** because you are trying to stop something happening. If your signal and your close proximity haven't stopped it you need to do something about it like removing an object a pupil is playing with, making an explicit statement or moving the person to a different seat.

Control sequence 2

This follows on from *Control sequence 1* and can be used either if the first sequence doesn't seem to be working or on its own as the first sequence that you try.

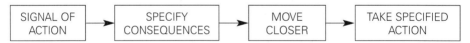

- **Signal of action** — this can be the same as in *Control sequence 1* but should be followed up with a stronger statement and a more assertive move towards the source of the problem, e.g. 'Don't do that' or 'I don't want you to do that again' or more specific 'I don't want you to tap your pen on the desk again'.
- **Specify consequences** — as you move forward, you make it clear what the consequences are if the behaviour continues, i.e. 'If you carry on doing that (specify what it is you don't like) this will happen (specify what exactly will happen)'.
- **Move closer** — this should be done at the same time as you are signalling and specifying the consequences.
- **Take specified action** — if the behaviour continues you must do something about it. You have said what you will do — now do it!

Control sequence 3

It has already been suggested that it is important not to overreact to inappropriate behaviour. This control sequence aims to keep the management of the behaviour private rather than making it a public spectacle. Many pupils who behave inappropriately develop strategies for not learning and enjoy the attention they get both from adults and from their peers. If they are deprived of their audience they often find it embarrassing to have to talk about their behaviour to you on their own. In fact, it is a situation they would prefer to avoid.

- **Comment to pupil** — this is similar to but a variation of 'signal of action' and 'move closer' in the earlier control sequences. You make a clear statement, preferably a calming yet assertive one such as, 'I don't like it when you do that' or 'I will not let you do that again'.
- **Specify consequences** — this is the same as in *Control sequence 2*.
- **Follow-up comment** — if the inappropriate behaviour has stopped this can be praise, for example, 'That's really good, I am pleased that you have stopped doing (specify what it was).' If it hasn't stopped you need to state what is going to happen and do it, e.g. send him/her out of the room, to another teacher etc.
- **Private discussion** — this can be extremely useful and should be a direct follow-up of the incident. It needs to take place between you and the pupil. A good way to approach this is to put the pupil on the spot even more by asking questions such as, 'Why did you behave like that?' and/or 'What are you going to do to stop it happening again?' It is also an opportunity for you to specify the rewards for behaving well and the future sanctions for behaving badly.

Control sequence 4

Imagine a situation where what you have tried so far hasn't worked. This time, as well as trying to stop what the pupil is doing, you are actually taking instant punitive action and not waiting until later after a warning or after the kind of private discussion in *Control sequence 3*.

| SIGNAL OF ACTION | → | SPECIFY CONSEQUENCES | → | MOVE CLOSER | → | WITHDRAW PUPIL | → | PUNITIVE TIME OUT |

You will be familiar with the first three elements because you have used them before. But, it is always worth trying them again to see if they will work.

- **Withdraw pupil** — assume that there has been no improvement in the pupil's behaviour or that the inappropriate behaviour has escalated into a confrontation between two pupils or a pupil and a teacher. Whatever the original problem, it is important at this stage to remove the pupil from the classroom, or wherever it is that the confrontation is taking place.
- **Punitive time out** — is the kind of action that has to be taken when other control tactics haven't worked and it has to involve the classroom rules and sanctions and probably those of the wider school community. The pupil must be isolated because his/her behaviour is so unacceptable. There must be a punishment in line with the school's wider policies and there certainly must be some serious discussions between the pupil and adults, which should include senior teachers such as year and department heads and the pupil's parents if appropriate.

Control sequence 5

This final sequence is slightly different from the previous four and doesn't necessarily follow on from them. It can be applied to poor behaviour but is probably better used to help pupils who are distracting themselves and others because they are finding the work that has been set too difficult.

| OFFER HELP | → | INTERVENE WITH HELP | → | CHANGE THE WORK | → | FIND FURTHER HELP |

- **Offer help** — sometimes inappropriate behaviour can be the result of boredom because the pupil finds the work too difficult or he/she cannot understand what has to be done. Sometimes very able and talented pupils can behave badly because of boredom linked to work that is too easy. You should offer help in the most unobtrusive way possible.

- **Intervene with help** — this takes the sequence a step further by beginning to help the pupil in whatever way is appropriate.
- **Change the work** — this time the pupil is helped directly, perhaps with different work altogether. The ability to differentiate the work accurately and in a well-planned way is essential.
- **Find further help** — learning difficulties resulting in bad behaviour might need outside help. You must draw on the school's systems and work closely with the special educational needs coordinator (SENCo).

Pupil strategies, teacher strategies

Both you and your pupils are trapped in situations where neither of you has much choice about who works with whom. Some pupils are able to develop many strategies for surviving on their own terms and unfortunately, these hardly ever relate to learning and good behaviour. This section describes some of their strategies, which you will probably find irritating. This is followed by a list of strategies you can use to overcome these barriers to learning. You will be able to use some of them more effectively than others and some, of course, will work better than others in your specific situation.

Pupil strategies

- Pupils often ask for reasons, which is not a problem if they are genuinely asking about what the work involves or where it fits into what they did last week etc. More often than not, however, it is done in a petulant, bored whine, saying things like: 'Why are we doing this?' or 'Do we really need to do this?' or 'This is boring'.
- Some pupils survive by being comedians and making other pupils laugh at inappropriate times and for the wrong reasons. They can be extremely funny — so beware — and don't laugh.
- Some pupils are attention seekers in other ways. They constantly seek reassurance by asking questions about their work to which they already know the answers and/or they constantly seek reassurance about whether their work is of the right standard or is what they were asked to do.
- Pupils can often trap themselves into irritating behaviour patterns such as always needing to be the first into the room or the first out of the room, the one who sulks if they give the wrong answer or the one who pretends indifference to anything new and exciting that is happening in school.
- Wasting time to avoid finishing or even starting work is quite common. It might mean frequent visits to the toilet, gossiping, constantly correcting and re-correcting their work.
- Some pupils seem immune to any sanctions or rewards and adopt an indifferent attitude to both.

Teacher strategies

These might include:
- negotiating and explaining to pupils what you are doing and why
- discussing with pupils what they are doing and what you are asking them to do
- using humour and jokes as motivating strategies
- making sure that all pupils are working hard and are continuously on-task in every lesson
- being willing and flexible enough to change tack and negotiate your lesson plan when and where necessary
- rewarding pupils publicly who work well
- appealing to pupils' better natures
- being assertive

Skills summary

This chapter emphasises how important it is to support pupils when they are learning and to establish the kinds of relationship that encourage learning. The key to making this successful is:
- assertive teaching
- assertive body language

It is also important to manage behaviour, and two simple procedures are identified that can be practised:
- using your eyes and being aware of everything that is happening
- using a series of control sequences

The final point is that pupils are not passive. They will develop all kinds of strategies to avoid working and to avoid the kind of effort you want them to make. You have to develop strategies to make them want to learn.

Activity 5.1

Relationships questionnaire

Read each statement and respond in the following way:

O = I behave in this way *often*
S = I behave in this way *sometimes*
N = I *never* behave in this way

Which of the following describe your teaching behaviour?

Arrive before the lesson is due to start	
Arrive well prepared and well planned	
Expect to give and receive respect	
Treat everyone as an individual	
Smile and say hello to the pupils in the class/tutor group	
Expect the occasional problem pupil as an inevitable part of teaching	
Listen when pupils are talking to you	
Use punishment sparingly	
Set high standards	
Apply rules fairly and consistently	
Deal with all misbehaviour	
Extend and motivate all pupils	
Enjoy yourself	
Enjoy teaching pupils who find learning difficult	
Display a good cross-section of pupils' work	
Avoid confrontation wherever possible	
Avoid humiliating pupils	
Avoid overreacting	
Avoid blanket punishments, i.e. punishing the whole class/tutor group for the bad behaviour of one or two pupils	
Avoid punishing more than you praise	
Avoid sarcasm and put downs	

Activity 5.2

More effective relationship skills

Read the statements below, tick the box that most applies to what you do and ask yourself:

- Why having this skill will make it easier to establish positive relationships.
- Why it will be difficult to establish positive relationships if you don't have this skill.

An effective teacher will...	Not often	Often	Very often
know each pupil's name, friends and personality			
be flexible and able to take advantage of unexpected events in a pupil's life, such as a new baby, return from an exotic holiday, broken arm etc.			
know what is happening in the classroom by moving around and being 'all seeing'			
plan and organise in such a way that time is used well and learning opportunities are maximised			
arrange the classroom furniture and space so that all pupils find it easy to move and easy to find their own space to work			
match work effectively to pupils' abilities			
pace lessons well so that there are no negatively pressurised rushes and no periods of inaction			
model the kind of polite and acceptable behaviour that will encourage good relationships			
improve relationships by using reprimands sparingly — but meaning them when they are used			
always try to criticise the behaviour rather than the person			
avoid using group punishments by being capable of finding the right culprit			
be firm, fair and consistent and reprimand pupils privately rather than publicly			

Activity 5.3

Assertive, aggressive or passive?

Relate each of the following words to a teaching style. Code each word as follows:

AS = assertive

AG = aggressive

PA = passive

Angry	
Confident	
Timid	
Quiet	
Out of control	
Put upon	
Hot tempered	
Fair	
Thoughtful	
Knowledgeable	
Volatile	
Lacking confidence	
Firm	
Mild	
Complaisant	
In control	
Dominant	
Violent	
Meek	
Dependent	

Activity 5.4

Step-by-step guide to assertion

> **Scenario**

---

1 SUMMARISE the behaviour that created the problem simply, unemotionally and straightforwardly.

---

2 STATE exactly how you feel, not how anyone else feels.

---

3 DESCRIBE clearly and simply why you feel like this.

---

4 SYMPATHISE or EMPATHISE with the pupil's point of view.

---

5 SPECIFY exactly what you would like the pupil to do. You must also say what you would be willing to do to find a solution, a compromise or a way out of the current situation.

---

6 DECIDE what your response will be. It is important that whatever you decide should clarify your position and not threaten the pupil.

Activity 5.5

Three teaching styles

Read each statement and rate each one using the following scale:
5 = a technique that you use frequently
3 = a technique you sometimes use
1 = a technique or style you hardly ever use

Group 1

Demands instant obedience	
Tells pupils what to do	
Uses a forbidding tone of voice most, if not all, of the time	
Uses threats	
Hardly ever gives choices	
Uses a bank of stock phrases such as: 'What do you think you are doing?', 'How dare you do that!' etc.	
Nags	
Often makes unrealistic demands by treating all pupils the same	
Is hostile and aggressive when disruption occurs	
Total	

Group 2

Communicates directly and assertively	
Achieves obedience without lowering self-esteem	
Is respectful even when driven to anger	
Tries not to react to incidents as they arise but, if possible, has a planned strategy	
Demands eye contact from a close distance but doesn't encroach on a pupil's personal space	
Speaks clearly, firmly and politely	
Always tries to distinguish between the person and the disruptive incident	
Expects obedience	
After a disruptive incident always gets back to the original working relationship	
Total	

Group 3

Uses body language in a non-assertive way	
In dealing with a disruptive incident often uses a prolonged dialogue with the pupil	
Often gives pupils the feeling that it is wrong to tell them what to do	
Doesn't use a forceful tone of voice	
Often gets angry and yells	
Feels guilty about getting angry and shouting	
Sees disruption as unusual and threatening giving a feeling of failure	
Often allows pupils to decide on the teacher's expectations of good behaviour	
Hopes that friendliness is enough to ensure good relationships	
Total	

When you have completed all three groups, total your score for each of the groups.

If you scored highest in *group 1*, you are more likely to be an **authoritarian** teacher.
If you scored highest in *group 2*, you are likely to be a **decisive** teacher.
If you scored highest in *group 3,* you are likely to be an **indecisive** teacher.
If you didn't score significantly higher in one group than in the others you use a mixture of styles.

6 Dealing with general teaching issues

As an effective teacher you will plan what you are going to do — you will know what you are going to teach and you will also have a good idea of what the pupils you are teaching will actually learn. At the same time you will also know what your reaction is going to be if any pupil or group of pupils misbehaves, fails to put in the required effort or has problems in learning and coping with what you want to teach. This will mean that your responses are measured and pre-planned and are much more likely to work than rapid knee-jerk reactions to any of the problems that you are likely to face. Many of the strategies in this chapter can be part of your overall planning process. As they concentrate on some common, general issues, they may overlap with earlier suggestions, run parallel to them or complement other tactics in some way.

Reducing stress, raising self-esteem and building confidence

It is important to support pupils who have low self-esteem because they will probably be the most vulnerable and may raise all kinds of barriers that prevent them from learning effectively. Before you can work on raising self-esteem, however, you will need to briefly look again at how you can create an appropriate classroom atmosphere.

First of all, Hughes (1999) states that all classrooms should be:
1 physically comfortable
2 welcoming
3 relaxing
4 reassuring and emotionally safe
5 stimulating and motivating
6 informative
7 interactive
8 attractive and cheerful
9 creative
10 surprising

Does this describe the classrooms that you teach in? If it doesn't, what changes could you make? **Activity 6.1** (p. 124) repeats the ten statements leaving spaces for you to think about how you can make your classroom match each of the statements. If you work in classrooms that fit the criteria you also need to make sure that the following six factors are in place because they are more likely to create a climate that reduces pupil stress and raises self-esteem:

1 **Freedom from physical harm** — this commits you to minimising violence, bullying and fighting.
2 **The absence of intimidation and fear** — this covers such things as emotional and non-verbal teasing and bullying.
3 **Recognising pupils as individuals** — each pupil needs to feel that they are an individual with their own place in the school.
4 **Belonging** — no pupil should feel alienated from what the school and the teaching group has to offer.
5 **Able to learn** — everyone needs to feel capable of learning and achieving without a sense of failing.
6 **The future** — life has to have some kind of meaning and pupils should have goals beyond school.

If the above six strategies are present in your classroom, you will need to maintain them. Here are what I feel are the ten most important strategies:

1 **Set clear objectives** — uncertainty can increase the level of stress in the classroom. Pupils need to know exactly what they will be doing and what will be expected of them within appropriate time limits.
2 **Circulate** — do not sit or stand still in the classroom unless you are working for a short time with an individual or a small group. Circulate so that you can monitor what every pupil is doing and so that everyone knows that they are being monitored. No one should think that they can hide in the classroom or do anything without you knowing about it.
3 **Set an example** — if you lean on a radiator in the classroom, making loud comments, picking your nose and laughing at anyone who makes a mistake, your pupils will think that this is acceptable behaviour. You need to be calm, professional, courteous, enthusiastic, polite, patient and well organised so that you provide a good example to all your pupils.
4 **Use non-verbal signals** — save your voice and don't shout unless it is extremely important to do so. Use as many non-verbal signals as possible to communicate what you want, such as: smiles, frowns, raised eyebrows, standing close and putting a finger on your lips.
5 **Use the teaching space creatively** — it is a good idea to change the seating arrangements and where pupils sit occasionally. It is equally important to create a vibrant, stimulating and colourful classroom where pupils feel that an effort has been made to welcome them.

6 **Low-level discipline** — low-level discipline problems, such as pupils talking when they are supposed to be working, the occasional shouted answer instead of raised hands etc. need to be tackled instantly with a policy of zero tolerance. Your intervention in these cases should be as quiet and as calm as possible with special attention being paid to anticipating problems before they escalate. Low-level intervention could mean mentioning a pupil's name, using an appropriate non-verbal cue such as a shake of the head, or stating clearly, calmly and assertively something like, 'Stop doing that immediately!'

7 **Assertive teaching** — as already described, this is about having the right attitude. It is also about setting clear behaviour boundaries and having the ability to assert power in any situation involving inappropriate behaviour.

8 **The egocentric 'I' teacher** — this is closely linked to being an assertive teacher and is about what you actually say when being assertive. You need to make clear statements about what it is that you want to happen. Examples might include: 'I expect you to...' or 'I want you to...' or 'I never want you to...'. By making straightforward, short and demanding 'I' statements you are making it clear what you want and making it more difficult for pupils to raise the stakes and start arguing about what they are doing or denying that their behaviour is inappropriate.

9 **Being human and rational** — this is about even more assertive 'I' messages and is part of the step-by-step guide to assertion. It is a fluid way of stating exactly what you want without leaving the situation open to escalation. An example might include describing the problem behaviour, stating the kind of effect it has and saying what will happen if it continues — 'Calling out instead of putting your hand up makes me angry. It interrupts the class and stops me teaching. Do it again and... (state what sanction will operate)'.

10 **Thinking positively** — this entails trying to change the negative to the positive and is sometimes difficult to do. It involves looking at the rules and regulations that operate in the school and trying to change them to reflect a positive view. Instead of a rule that says 'No running in the classroom' — simply change it to 'Always walk in the classroom'. It is a way of stating exactly what you expect but with a shift in emphasis towards a more positive approach.

You will have come across pupils who experience huge amounts of failure. Many of them will have low self-esteem and they will have learned how to erect all kinds of barriers that will prevent them from learning. Below is a list of strategies for boosting pupils' confidence in who they are and what they need to learn:

- You need to show pupils that you believe in them and that you know it is worthwhile working with them.
- They will need lots of praise and instant feedback for any of their successes.
- Focus on their strengths rather than on their weaknesses and try to use their strengths to help you teach them and to help them learn.

- Encourage as much independence as possible so that they will learn to try out new things.
- Make sure that the challenges you set pupils with low self-confidence — in terms of the work they are expected to do — are achievable.
- Try to avoid negative remarks — it is very easy to say something disparaging without really meaning to.
- Give your pupils lots of opportunities to succeed and show them how to build on their successes.

Strategies to prevent bullying

No one deserves to be bullied. Yet despite all the anti-bullying policies in schools, 46% (nearly half) of all secondary pupils say that it has happened to them. In a wider context, the National Workplace Bullying Survey (TUC Health and Safety Executive, November 2005) reported that 2 million people had been bullied at work in the previous 6 months, that 47% of British employees had witnessed bullying at work, that 34% of those bullied at work had made a formal complaint but just 5% said their actions resolved the problem while 27% said it made the situation worse. And all these figures are linked to another depressing adult statistic — by the age of 24, 60% of identified bullies have a criminal conviction.

So bullying can be everywhere; before school and after school, as children and as adults. It is a problem that extends far beyond the classroom. You can help change attitudes and can support victims and their parents, but you can't do it on your own. Maybe the *Every Child Matters* initiative will bring together parents, police, teachers, health workers and social services to help tackle the wider social implications of bullying. But as a teacher, you will have to take the initiative by adopting a zero-tolerance policy to bullying.

Bullying is the systematic victimisation of another person. It is the illegitimate use of power to hurt someone and can include: name calling, teasing, racist taunting, taking money or possessions, threatening reprisals, damaging possessions, physical violence and rude, threatening and/or obscene gestures. It even extends to the use of text messages on mobile phones and to e-mails. Every adult and pupil connected to the school needs to know that bullying is treated seriously. This is an admirable concept but it relies on everyone recognising what bullying is, telling someone that it is happening and knowing that something will be done about it. There has to be an ethos of 'telling' and an anti-bullying policy that pervades every corner of the school and is part of the curriculum, the rewards and sanctions system, assemblies and the work of the school council. It has to be seen to be high profile, with posters, peer pressure and support systems, buddy schemes, assertiveness programmes, counselling and mediation schemes. Parents of bullies must know what is happening and must expect to be called in for meetings. Similarly, the parents of victims must understand what is being done to help their child. No part of the school must be seen as a no-go area by teachers or as their own territory by pupils. Breaktimes and lunchtimes must be strictly supervised so that bullies and potential bullies recognise that their lives are being made difficult and that all teachers and adults have the skills and the determination to deal with them.

Pupils who are likely to be bullies usually demonstrate assertive and aggressive attitudes over which they have little control. They often feel insecure, inadequate and humiliated and may have been bullied at home. They are often encouraged by parents to overreact violently, to bear grudges and to adopt a hard, menacing attitude. As they lack empathy, they can't imagine what their victim feels like and frequently rationalise that they somehow deserve to be bullied. These are severe problems and show how difficult it is, not only to prevent bullying in the first place, but to change the behaviour of those who are doing it. No one finds it easy to like a bully, but it is possible to see how they need their own kinds of support.

Pupils who are victims are usually nervous or anxious, and may be new to the school, different in speech, appearance and/or background. Sometimes potential victims also demonstrate what bullies may see as amusing and entertaining reactions such as tantrums or loss of control. Victims are by their very nature vulnerable and many go out of their way to avoid any contact with potential bullies.

Quite often, bullies and some of their victims are part of the same marginalised and friendless group. Some victims can change their role within their group of 'friends' from victim to bully depending on who they are interacting with. Parents of the 'victim' can make the situation more difficult by complaining about bullying and then failing to see their own child's role in the problem when, under different circumstances and with different 'friends', they become tomorrow's bully. This also makes it even more difficult for teachers who will have problems finding out the truth and, by implication, finding out who the actual bully is.

If the telling ethos of the school works, most incidents will be reported, but on some occasions it will be necessary to recognise the signs of victimisation. Many victims begin to perform poorly in school work and are unwilling to go to school or are frightened of walking to and from school. Bullying may mean that they have unexplained bruises or scratches, or that they arrive home with property or clothes dirty or damaged, or that they are hungry because their lunch has been stolen or damaged. They will want to be close to adults and to secure parts of the building during breaks, may have a poor appetite at home, cry themselves to sleep and have nightmares and be so frightened that they refuse to say what is wrong. Adults in school have to be able to link these patterns of behaviour to what is causing it.

When confronted by bullying don't be shocked into knee-jerk reactions and ways of initiating draconian punishments. Immediate action does need to be taken but you need to think about long-term changes. Some immediate strategies include:

- Staying calm — reacting loudly and emotionally may increase the bully's fun. Bullies can handle you being tough and angry.
- Let the bully and the victim know that you are taking the incident seriously. In fact, make it clear to the bully when and why you are being punitive.
- It might be useful to try and develop some peer-group pressure against the bully and their actions.
- Reassure the victim and prevent them from blaming themselves or feeling inadequate or foolish. Offer them immediate advice and support and discuss what you are doing with their parents. Consider offering some assertiveness training.
- Try to encourage the bully to empathise and see the victim's point of view. It is useful to involve the bully's parents, although the parents may feel that the behaviour you are so concerned about is relatively normal.
- If the victim is in agreement, set up a bullying court where the victim, with friends in support, confront the bully and state exactly what the bully has done and what effect it has had.

At the same time as you are taking action, i.e. doing something about it, remember that certain actions may make the bullying worse, or at best fail to help stop it in any meaningful way.

Some of the **don'ts** include:

- Don't attack the individual pupil or his/her behaviour. Remember, bullies really do thrive on power, aggression and anger and will see any personal attack as a challenge.
- Don't react as if the bully is a personal affront to you. This will just be seen as another challenge or even a personal victory for the bully.
- Don't publicly put down a bully or he/she will either seethe with resentment, which could make his/her behaviour worse, or see the put-down as yet another challenge and battle to be won.
- Don't say things like, 'Other people won't like you if you bully them, you know'. This won't work because it reinforces the kind of negative attention that bullies thrive on.
- Don't neglect a bully's self-esteem and his/her learning needs.

Once short-term action has been taken, find out what triggered the incident and whether there are more 'quick fix' actions that can be taken. For example, there may be issues related to how well the grounds or toilets are being supervised; you and your colleagues may need more training; the number of lunchtime supervisors may need to be increased, or some pupils may need excluding.

Violence and aggression

In every school, including yours, there will be pupils who use unacceptable violence and who use their physical strength through hitting, slapping, kicking, punching etc. to dominate other pupils and establish their power base. Many pupils who behave in this way are bullies. Others, however, may commit random acts of violence that are not part of any systematic intimidation of one person but just how they feel that they should conduct social relationships within their peer group. This kind of attitude can be reinforced at home and if this is the case, any attempts at discussing the problem with parents will be difficult. Such pupils may also have low status at school with very little self-esteem. Violence and fighting might be prevented by trying some of the following approaches:

- There should be a series of whole-school and classroom rules that relate to violence of any kind with a strict hierarchy of sanctions and punishments.
- If you have to deal with unacceptable violence stay calm and don't give the participants any clue as to how angry you feel. You should give the impression of being totally in control.
- Ask questions so that you have to be given a verbal and not a physical response.
- The questions should be framed so that they begin to calm down a volatile situation and make the pupil start taking decisions that will get him/her out of the situation he/she is in. For example, 'Aren't you already in enough trouble?' or, 'Why don't you stop fighting now before you get into even more trouble?'
- Talk to each fighter separately, never together or they will shout and contradict each other. Remember, emotions are running high.
- Make it absolutely clear to pupils and their parents that any kind of violence or fighting in school will not be allowed.
- Establish clear behaviour goals for pupils who are violent and set up behaviour-monitoring schemes. They may also need the help of outside support agencies.
- Talk to such pupils about alternative courses of action and different ways of solving problems. A trained counsellor would be good at this.
- When violent pupils do not react aggressively they need to be praised and rewarded in some way.
- It is sometimes useful to make the participants in a fight write down what happened and why. These written statements can be used in the discussions that you have with them.
- Try making him/her feel guilty by saying something like, 'I am really disappointed in you and I hate to see you getting into trouble...'.

At the same time, it is important not to allow the problem to escalate by including some or all of the following:

- Don't refuse to listen to pupils who are involved in fights or violent acts.
- Don't always focus on the pupil's negative behaviour. Try and find something positive that he/she does.
- Telling a violent pupil that he/she is 'stupid', a 'violent thug' or a 'violent, mindless idiot' will not help solve his/her problem.
- It is important not to be seen to dislike the person who is violent. It can be difficult, but a professional attitude must be adhered to.

Aggression is similar to but not always quite the same as violence and fighting. It can include over-competitive behaviour, intimidation through shouting and belligerence, confrontation, pushing and threatening. It has similar results, however — you will be distracted by what the aggressive pupil is doing and the affect he/she is having on other pupils. It is important that you don't reflect the pupil's aggressive behaviour by being aggressive in return. Because aggressive pupils are very competitive and can't bear to lose, it is equally important not to feel that you have to 'win' each confrontation. Dealing with such pupils, especially if there is more than one in a class, is far from easy. Some suggestions include:

- Stay calm (this has been emphasised over and over again) and try to slow any situation down. You need to prevent the aggressive pupil from getting anything out of a confrontation.
- Talk to aggressive pupils (on their own, remember) in an attempt to show them that there are other ways of trying to solve problems.
- One-to-one discussions are vitally important, with no audience to provoke more aggression.
- Make sure that you raise such issues as: calmness, backing away from situations, talking through disputes and not upsetting others.
- When confronting such pupils with their behaviour (in your one-to-one discussions), make sure that you are as precise as possible. Rather than, 'I want to talk about the problem you had with Jane at lunchtime'. Change this to, 'I want to talk about why you shouted in Jane's face and pushed her against the wall at lunchtime'.
- As with all other behaviour issues, praise positive behaviour.
- Giving aggressive pupils time to calm down and cool off is important.
- Think about counselling. Aggressive pupils could have personality problems and may be unpopular with their peers. It might be possible to change this through regular counselling sessions.
- Pupils who are aggressive can easily lose control and behave unpredictably. This kind of reaction, which can be similar to a tantrum, makes them impossible to reason with until the reaction has stopped and they have calmed down. In a crowded classroom, this behaviour is difficult to handle and resolve because it is a very public display of disruption that is both threatening and distressing. It can also be entertaining and some pupils with their own difficulties

may find such distractions amusing, which may mean that they provoke a reaction as often as possible. It is important to try to identify what causes the loss of control, and if there are certain predictable incidents that trigger a reaction you will need to minimise them. At the same time, talk to the class about the problem (when the actual problem pupil is out of the room) and talk about strategies to avoid confrontations and loss of control. This kind of disruptive, time-consuming and energy-sapping behaviour stops you teaching and other pupils from learning so it can't be allowed to happen on a regular basis and must not be allowed to impact on raising standards.

Teaching creatively

Creativity is becoming part of the educational psyche and the government is beginning to recognise that young people need to develop the creative skills required in the workplace of the future. Fast-moving technology and the increasing demands of flexibility and imagination mean that all pupils need to be able to pose questions such as 'what if...?', 'perhaps if...?', 'why?' and 'why not?' It is more than likely that they will change jobs several times and this will mean that they will need to have the ability to cope with change and come up with creative solutions in more and more complex situations. Creative teaching will help increase pupils' ability to solve problems, think independently and work flexibly. It also might mean that those pupils who are disaffected in any way might come to realise that what is being offered by you and the school is useful.

The Qualifications and Curriculum Authority (QCA) has published *Creativity: Find it, Promote it* (www.ncaction.org.uk/creativity/). At the same time, an Ofsted publication entitled *Expecting the Unexpected: Developing Creativity in Primary and Secondary Schools* (www.ofsted.gov.uk) suggests that 'being creative' and 'creative teaching' are not radical or new concepts; all they really involve is a willingness to observe, listen and work closely with pupils to help them develop their ideas in a purposeful way. The report also suggests that it is vital for school leadership to be committed to promoting creativity across the whole school, because their support and encouragement will permit both you and your pupils to work creatively and, at the same time, ensure good practice is recognised, resourced properly and disseminated across the school.

Ofsted's *Expecting the Unexpected* suggests that creativity in schools has four characteristics:
1 thinking and behaving **imaginatively**
2 the imaginative activities take place in a **purposeful** way, i.e. related to a specific objective
3 the activity generates something **original**
4 there is **value** in the activity that is related to the original objective

This immediately removes any vague ideas that creativity is about lying in the sun thinking 'creative' thoughts that are never realised. Although this kind of day-dreaming can be part of a creative process, creative people actually do something. They are purposeful. They have an objective, whether it is an original recipe, a design for a bridge, a great painting or a beautiful poem.

Creativity needs to be a whole-school issue. The National Advisory Committee on Creative and Cultural Education (NACCCE) is amassing a considerable amount of data which suggest that the more engaged your pupils are in creative activities, the better the behaviour and the higher their achievements. Ofsted's *Expecting the Unexpected* notes that the most effective schools:

- have the development of creativity high on any list of priorities
- are outward looking, welcoming and open to ideas from external agencies
- demonstrate no radical new teaching methods, but pupils' ideas are developed in a purposeful way

Perhaps the most significant issue is that by encouraging your pupils to be creative you are encouraging them to think for themselves in ways that should elicit high achievement and a certain amount of freedom of thought. If you value and encourage creativity you will be able to:

- provide an environment where pupils go beyond the expected and are reward-ed for doing so
- help pupils find a personal relevance in learning activities
- create a stable and structured ethos for a successful curriculum but at the same time create alternatives in the way information is taught and shared
- encourage pupils to examine and explore alternative ways of doing things
- give them time for this kind of exploration

Creativity should be at the centre of the curriculum, and time, resources and professional development opportunities should be available to make it effective. Generating enthusiasm among your colleagues and pupils can be difficult. I would favour the big bang theory rather than the dripping tap where creativity only filters slowly through the school. Why not consider involving the whole school in a week-long cross-curricular creative event that culminates with assemblies and displays of examples of pupils' creativity to which parents and other members of the community are invited? This is difficult to organise in a crowded timetable that is structured to a tight curriculum — but not impossible if you do the following:

- Timetable lessons so that they can be changed and adjusted easily.
- Allow long blocks of time for creativity, e.g. a half day or whole day instead of the usual shorter blocks of time for lessons.
- Challenge yourselves to develop creative teaching strategies.
- Develop better resources and working conditions so that pupils have access to

materials, tools and spaces such as dance studios, music labs and computer suites.

- Invite in creative artists such as actors, musicians, painters, computer software and games designers to run workshops.
- Involve pupils in changing the environment — this can range from better and more creative displays to working with outside agencies to change parts of the site by improving outside areas.
- Use the school community. Ask around and you will find teachers, teaching assistants, parents and governors who have all kinds of creative talents that they will be willing to use as part of the school's creativity drive.

As part of your continuing professional development you may need training in creativity and it will need to be part of your performance management targets. If creativity is part of a staff development programme everyone is more likely to be enthusiastic. One of the most important points to make is that creativity won't just arrive and settle in your classroom and become instantly successful. Like everything else that is effective, you have to plan for it to happen. It might be possible for existing teaching styles, schemes of work and medium and short-term plans to be modified in some way so that there is more potential for creativity. But, it might also be the case that you will have to modify your approach and promote a range of teaching and learning styles that will allow many more pupils to demonstrate their creativity.

A creative teacher should:

- encourage open-ended questioning and promote and reward imagination and originality
- increase the use of role play, hands-on experimentation, problem solving and collaborative group work
- create conditions for adventurous exploration of ideas as well as those for quiet reflection and concentration
- where appropriate use unexpected events and put aside what had been planned to go with some new idea without losing sight of the original broad objectives
- be willing to stand back and let pupils take the lead

The QCA document, *Creativity: Find it, Promote it*, offers a positive conclusion when it suggests that pupils who are encouraged to be creative and independent become more interested in discovering things, more open to new ideas, keener to explore new ideas and are even willing to work beyond lesson time. If you promote creativity you will make sure that all pupils respond positively to opportunities, challenges and responsibilities and are better able to cope with new challenges as well as with change and adversity.

Zero tolerance

Zero tolerance has been part of the vocabulary used in fighting crime for several years. It has now, through several secretaries of state for education, also become part of the wider debate on behaviour and negative attitudes to learning in schools. This is partly because of the current view of the Chief Inspector of Schools that, despite an Ofsted inspection framework that has been in place for many years, a significant number of schools are still underperforming and not raising standards because many of these schools are not managing behaviour properly and, as a consequence, pupils are unable to learn effectively.

I have already argued that there should be no tolerance to bullying, violence and any kind of major classroom misbehaviour, but the current use of the term 'zero tolerance' can also be applied to what has come to be known as low-level class-room disruption. This includes such things as talking over the teacher, answering back, casual rudeness to other pupils and teachers, disobeying any instruction, laughing inappropriately, shouting and calling out etc. It is the kind of behaviour that makes being able to teach effectively difficult, if not impossible, and which has a debilitating and stressful effect on any teacher who has to deal with it day in and day out. It is also the kind of behaviour that successful teachers have never, ever tolerated although for some reason, in some schools it has become acceptable and is often seen as inevitable.

It seems to me that there has to be 'zero tolerance' of any behaviour that prevents teachers teaching and pupils learning and that this has to be made clear as a whole-school policy. At the same time, it cannot just be a policy that exists on paper. It must be part of a wide range of teaching skills and a clear and decisive part of whole-school behaviour policy. It has to fit into how the school's behaviour policy works, how sanctions are operated, what rules exist, what sanctions are used, how pupils are dealt with when they break rules, how the school's behaviour policy is communicated to parents and pupils, how they are rewarded for good behaviour and all the other strategies relating to such things as diet and exercise. In other words, it cannot exist on its own as just a brave statement of intent.

To use zero tolerance supportively and effectively, there has to be an appropriate overall ethos within which it can neatly fit as part of the school's, and by impli-cation your, overall strategy. Many psychologists identify four broadly different styles of teacher–pupil relationships in schools (remember authoritative and authoritarian?) They are:

- **Authoritative** — where pupils are cared for and supported within very firm boundaries. Within those boundaries there is a certain amount of freedom but you will mean what you say and will not shy away or back down when enforcing the tight limits you have set.

- **Authoritarian** — where there is a less caring and supportive element and less response to individual needs. There will be expectations for pupils to obey strict instructions without any explanation.
- **Indulgent** — where, in terms of rules and behaviour management, you will be undemanding and permissive and set few clear boundaries. Sanctions will hardly ever exist let alone be used and pupils will look as if they are in control.
- **Uninvolved** — where, as well as being undemanding and permissive with few clear boundaries in terms of behaviour, you will not really care very much. You will do little monitoring of behaviour and the feeling will be that you are unresponsive to the pupils' needs.

Obviously, how the four styles work will involve some degree of overlap but where zero tolerance exists it has a better chance of success and acceptance in a school with an 'authoritative' ethos. It needs to be part of a system where there are tight boundaries with known consequences and sanctions that operate immediately every time there is misbehaviour within a supportive and caring atmosphere. This puts a great deal of pressure on whole schools and departments and on you as an individual teacher to be very clear in explaining this approach to parents and pupils. However, once all those who have a vested interest in maintaining good behaviour see it working, they will also see more contented teachers, happier pupils who are able to learn without disruption and, of course, a rise in standards.

The public perception seems to be that behaviour and attitudes to learning in schools and individual classrooms is scandalously bad and that bullying is rife, with no pupil being safe because of drugs, guns, knives and general mayhem. Schools do not exist within a vacuum and there are all kinds of negative social influences. Schools are expected to deal with the day-to-day effects of bad behaviour by the same society that fails to condemn spitting and swearing footballers and considers rude 'celebrities' to be so interesting that they fill the tabloids. How can schools change this culture of lack of respect and acceptance of disruptive behaviour? It is with this backdrop that zero tolerance is now part of the debate on behaviour in schools.

Zero tolerance needs to be applied to *all* negative attitudes in *all* schools. Pupils need to know what is acceptable behaviour and what will be treated with zero tolerance. Although some of the following points may be contentious, a policy of zero tolerance should include the following:

- **The street has no place in the school** — strict school uniform should be enforced, with no one allowed to wear anything that smacks of street or gang culture. If pupils don't wear the appropriate clothes, they should be sent home. Sending pupils home causes parents problems and may make them see that their child conforms next time.

- **Technology in the school is used for the school** — no mobile phones should be used or even switched on in lessons, and no misuse made of the school's computer network. As in the workplace, the consequences of abusing this should be severe and in the case of the school, lead to exclusion.
- **Parents do have a responsibility** — parents should be called into school to sit with their disruptive children. If this means loss of earnings, so be it.
- **This classroom is my classroom** — teachers should be in charge of everything that happens in their teaching space, directing pupils into their classroom, telling them where to sit and indicating appropriate behaviour.
- **Instant help** — there should be instant support and instant systems of withdrawal and detention for pupils who behave badly. Behaving badly in this context is not just about extreme behaviour but is about good manners and respect.
- **School is a civilised place** — civilised behaviour should be expected. The rules of behaviour should be the same in every classroom with systems in place to help everyone. Swearing, violence and all identified low-level disruption will have its consequences.
- **The teachers have rights** — teachers and teaching assistants *must not* be subjected to sexist or racist comments or sexual innuendo. They must not be sworn at or threatened in any way. Pupils who do this will be removed from the classroom and, if any threats or behaviours that have been made are breaches of the law and illegal, then they should be removed from the school and the police informed.
- **Instant exclusion** — this should happen in instances of violence or significant threats. Exclusions of this kind should mean that the pupil does not return to threaten any teacher again.

Many pupils have the wrong attitudes to learning and behave badly simply because they can. They get away with it once and do it again. The ideal system would be that they do it once and then don't get away with it. There are many pupils with dysfunctional families who do not have the same value systems as the school. But we need to be creating havens of good behaviour and we need to tell the world all about civilised values. There should be newsletters home, general meetings, more newsletters, individual letters home, letters about exclusions, and about detentions. There should be home–school agreements and the opportunity for all parents to use the school and to have access to a wide range of other agencies that can help them with any difficulties that they may be having. There needs to be a continuing dialogue between the school and all parents so that parents realise that they and the school probably want the same things for their children.

So far, the stick has been used to build a system where you are not left isolated to deal with problems in your classroom that disrupt learning. But zero tolerance and sanctions *will not* work unless they are used alongside reward systems mentioned in previous chapters:

- **Everyone can succeed** — the school should not be geared up to academic success alone (although this is extremely important). There are all kinds of activities such as sports, dance, ICT etc. where pupils can be rewarded both privately and quietly in their classrooms and loudly and publicly in whole-school events.

- **The 3-metre rule** — this might sound strange but it works. You and all adults working in school should speak to pupils in a positive way whenever they pass within 3 metres of them. This tells pupils that you feel positive, that you want to be there with them and that you are happy at the prospect of working with them. It is also good manners.

- **The no put-down zone** — pupils are good at sneering, criticising and generally 'putting down' contributions in the classroom or even jeering at different accents, clothes and attitudes. If you make the school a 'no put-down zone' this is not allowed. Once again this has to be a whole-school effort. If every put-down is commented on every time it happens, it doesn't take long for pupils to recognise what you mean and to start openly resenting other pupils' put-downs of themselves. It works best alongside a philosophy where blame is not attached to a pupil in a belittling way. Once the concept of no put-downs has been established, most pupils will be enthusiastic and recognise that it allows them to make mistakes without blame or ridicule.

- **Good food** — diet does affect behaviour. Why not take a direct stand and ban all highly sugared, highly coloured, additive-filled drinks or sweets both at lunchtime and in vending machines. It can be done.

- **A school fit for pupils** — shabby buildings will mean dispirited teachers and low standards. Fresh paint, carpets and good furniture will help everyone recognise that the school is a smart place to work in.

- **No hiding place** — there should be no secret places where pupils might feel afraid. The violent and the aggressive often see toilets as their private places. It is a good idea to make it a rule that every time teachers pass toilets they knock and go in to check. Once pupils know that this happens regularly, the space becomes everyone's again.

Activity 6.2 (p. 126) emphasises that the stick-and-carrot approach will work if each teacher is assertive enough to want to make their school a place where pupils actually want to be and work. It is worth completing as a way of thinking about how you and other colleagues can actually make this happen.

There are no quick answers, but schools that are good at managing behaviour have head teachers, senior managers and teachers who have created an ethos where pupils lose rather than gain popularity by causing trouble. These same teachers can spot a disruptive incident in the making and by using an appropriate tactic nip it in the bud. They understand how young people react to each other and to adults and are able to model the good behaviour they expect from their pupils. It isn't easy to achieve but is essential if we are to take our schools back from the violent and the disruptive.

Using teaching assistants effectively

It has been said that 'For every person wishing to teach, there are 30 not wanting to be taught'. This is all too often true. What can we do about it? Teaching assistants can play an important role in supporting teachers, helping them to manage the curriculum, working with pupils with SEN and emotional and behavioural difficulties (EBD) and reducing teachers' workloads.

Who are they and what do they do?

Teaching assistants, like teachers, come from a variety of backgrounds. Some will have a lot of experience of working in schools and some will be highly qualified in other fields. Whatever their backgrounds, they will all be a potential source of help and support. It makes sense for you to maximise their use, and show them how their role can be integrated into the day-to-day workings of a busy department and hectic classroom.

Teaching assistants are mainly expected to cover the following five areas:
- **Educational support** – the support that they give to teaching and the curriculum.
- **Pastoral support** – working with pupils who have emotional as well as behavioural and learning difficulties.
- **Liaising with colleagues** – helping to prepare lessons in conjunction with teachers and other assistants.
- **General ancillary duties** – carrying out routine tasks to support workload remodelling.
- **Duties relating to preparation, planning and assessment (PPA) time** – working with larger groups of pupils and doing many of the tasks associated with the above four areas.

If you do work with an assistant with some of your teaching groups you should benefit from sharing and developing each other's strengths. This will happen more effectively when you have someone whose qualities include flexibility, a sense of fairness, versatility, patience and an abundance of good humour. Some schools and departments find it easier to work with teaching assistants than others, and there are certain aspects of a school's or department's ethos and culture that will make sure that working alongside teaching assistants is about mutual professionalism and developing strategies along the following lines:

- **Using the School Improvement Plan** — to take decisions about how teaching assistants are best used, with whom and where.
- **Using performance management** — to support the professional needs of teaching assistants, setting appropriate targets for their development and matching their skills to the needs of the children and the school.
- **Including teaching assistants in the formal culture of the school** through planning meetings, decision-making groups and curriculum committees.
- **Including them in the informal culture of the school** — in the staffroom and social events.
- **Communicating with teaching assistants** — letting them know what is happening in terms of daily and weekly messages, including times of meetings.
- **Telling governors and parents** how important teaching assistants are in raising standards.
- **Celebrating achievement** — valuing their work by praising them and acknowledging their successes.
- **Recognising that they can provide:**
  - additional teaching and learning support
  - more effective teaching and learning for specific pupils with SEN
  - a more consistent approach to behaviour management
  - emotional support to teachers
  - local information and useful knowledge about the community

One of the main ways to use teaching assistants effectively is to share the planning of lessons with them. Finding time to do this is difficult but the key phrase is, 'If you can't learn to plan you won't plan to learn'. Planning together is an important part of the relationship between you and a teaching assistant. They need to know what the lesson objectives and the differentiated tasks are and they should also be aware of your expectations regarding the quality of the work, key assessment issues and acceptable noise levels in the classroom. It is possible to share all this information in a weekly meeting followed by short reminders immediately before each lesson.

The more teaching assistants know about each pupil that they are working with the better. If a teaching assistant is being used to support you, or if there are higher level teaching assistants (HLTAs) who are working with classes under minimal teacher supervision, their attention will need to be drawn to the ability levels of individuals as well as groups. This will mean identifying those of high ability as well as low ability and pointing out why certain pupils are put into certain learning groups. Those with EBD will find it difficult to learn and will achieve little if their fragile hold on patterns of behaviour is broken. Teaching assistants need to be used to support children with EBD, but to do this successfully, they need to know who they are and what tactics usually work.

Teaching assistants are being used increasingly to support teachers and need to be trained in many more of the skills that you have. They should *always* work under your supervision and you need to be confident that they have the necessary skills to do what they are expected to do. This is because they will not necessarily be always under your *direct* supervision and in the same teaching space. They will, within the changes that are taking place for planning, preparation and assessment (PPA) time, be expected to work with pupils on their own. When they do work in this way, it is essential that everyone — teachers, parents, governors and heads of department etc. — are confident that they can be used effectively.

The changes to how teaching assistants are used has meant that they must all be computer literate, familiar with the demands of the National Curriculum, especially numeracy and literacy, able to plan pupils' learning, assess pupils, manage their behaviour and, in many cases, support teachers in meetings and case conferences. This is a formidable list that underpins the growing professionalism of their role and the need to use them as fellow professionals.

Some final instant strategies

Several strategies are included here that reinforce earlier sections. All of them can be operated in isolation but will be more successful if used as part of a coherent policy to overcome negative attitudes and disruptive and inappropriate behaviour. These final strategies will be most useful if they are seen as ways of establishing routines and a sense of order so that pupils who are likely to want to misbehave have to make an effort to do so because of the orderly, work-orientated atmosphere. It is your job to make poor behaviour, disruption and inappropriate actions of any kind as difficult as possible by making it clear that such behaviour is not acceptable in your classroom and in their school. Instant strategies include:

- **Punctuality** — make this the norm in everything that happens in your classroom. You must arrive on time and so must your pupils. They must complete their work on time, homework must be handed in on time and lessons planned to fit the amount of time that is available.
- **Beginnings and ends of lessons** — start on time (punctuality) and make sure that all pupils are in the right place and are listening. Do not talk over pupils' conversations. Make sure that you set clear lesson objectives that the children know and can understand.
- **Motivation** — this is one of the keys to minimising disruption and raising achievement. You need to be able to challenge and motivate all pupils, not just

most of them. This is especially true of low achievers and those who are vulnerable with low self-esteem.

- **Noise level** — the level of noise in the classroom has to be related to the task in hand. Practical activities and group discussions etc. will generate more noise than pupils who are working individually on a set task. You have to establish clear rules about noise levels with fast and understood signals to bring it down to an acceptable level.
- **Keeping children on-task** — if pupils are not on-task, they will not be completing the work that has been set and may well be disruptive. Make sure that what they are learning is worthwhile and move around the room constantly reminding pupils about what they are supposed to be doing.
- **Learning strategies** — different pupils will respond to different teaching styles because they will have different learning styles. If there is no match between how the pupils in your class learn and how you are teaching, then there may be more disruption than is necessary.
- **Knowing your pupils** — it is important to know your pupils, especially those whose learning and perhaps behaviour is causing you concern. The more you know the more choices you will be able to make about what strategies to use.

Skills summary

Being an effective teacher means having a range of skills that you know will work in all kinds of different situations. It is far better to have strategies that you can use over and over again than to have to resort to rapid knee-jerk reactions that might not be appropriate, or work. This chapter identifies the areas where you need to be successful:

- building confidence and raising self-esteem
- strategies to prevent bullying, violence and aggression
- creative teaching
- zero tolerance
- using teaching assistants effectively

Activity 6.1

Developing the learning classroom

This is about how to make your classroom into a space where pupils find learning easier and are more confident about making the effort to raise their own standards and succeed.

Read each of the ten statements and use the boxes to write notes on how you can make this happen in your classroom. If possible share what you have said with a colleague who has also completed this sheet. If you agree that what you have written is important, how will you make it happen?

1 Physically comfortable

2 Welcoming

3 Relaxing

4 Reassuring and emotionally safe

5 Stimulating and motivating

6 Informative

7 Interactive

8 Attractive and cheerful

9 Creative

10 Surprising

Activity 6.2

Some essential factors in your classroom

Read each of the statements and then ask yourself:

- Is this happening in my classroom?
- If it is, how do I make it happen?
- If it isn't, how can I make it happen?

Use the boxes to make notes and, where possible, to share the information with colleagues.

---

1 Pupils are happy

---

2 They work hard

---

3 They are treated fairly

---

4 They receive help both academically and socially

---

5 There is a lively, creative atmosphere

6 Pupils are motivated

7 Discipline is positive and consistent

8 Everyone feels that it is their classroom and their school

7 Developing leadership skills and the search for promotion

I hope that by reading the earlier chapters and using the activities you have become a more assertive and effective teacher. If this is the case, you might be feeling ready to increase your overall responsibilities by taking on more leadership and management roles. This should mean promotion and more money and it will certainly mean more work, more demands on your time and the possibility of more stress. But, the rewards can be high. You will already be in demand as a successful teacher, and your knowledge and experience will help you to influence colleagues in their drive to raise standards.

Effective performance management reviews

Teachers in general don't like being observed and you, like all your colleagues, may feel that whoever is doing the watching is bound to find something to criticise. The whole process also conjures up images of Ofsted inspectors, clipboards, checklists and a fear of failure. Yet watching each other teaching should be a regular and normal part of school life as well as a positive learning experience.

Even in the most team-orientated schools, with the best support systems and a really well-developed culture of 'no blame', teachers will always be apprehensive about being observed. But classroom observation contributes to school improvement because you need to know what the quality of your teaching is like. Subject managers and heads of department have to be able to demonstrate that they know what the overall quality of the teaching in their department is like. The new Ofsted inspection framework insists that schools and departments are good at 'self-evaluation', which means that having a system of observing lessons in place to monitor teaching quality is essential. So, there has to be a system that works because watching each other teach is one of the most powerful tools available for professional development. This is true for both the person observing and the one being observed.

First of all, there needs to be a **focus for the observation**. This may be part of a whole-school or department focus, a subject focus or an element of concern expressed by the person being observed. Here are some examples.

Whole-school or department concerns will include:

- pace of lessons
- involvement of boys in lessons
- the use of praise to support reluctant girls
- effective use of support staff

Subject focus will include:

- use of questioning in numeracy
- how boys are encouraged in writing
- how SEN pupils are included in science investigations
- why the standards in specific parts of the curriculum are lower than other areas of the same subject

An individual's concerns will be:

- Can you look at whether I ask my low-ability boys enough questions?
- Do you think I offer enough praise to my high-ability pupils?
- How can I improve my discipline with three specific (named) boys?

There is an inevitable element of structure and formality which means that *even* this kind of peer observation isn't completely stress free — but, the more trust, the less stress. There is also a need for some kind of **formal record** of all observations as part of performance management so that there are details of the kinds of continuity and improvements that have been made. Record sheets need to be simple and easily understood. The one reproduced as **Activity 7.1** (p. 148) can be completed during a lesson observation.

Completing an observation and filling in an observation sheet is in itself not easy, but the most difficult part is at the end. There has to be time built into any performance management cycle for a **constructive discussion** because this is where you will learn so much from the observation that you will realise what a powerful learning tool it is. The post-observation discussion will help you move your expertise as well as your career forward because, first of all you will be discussing how effective your teaching is with a senior member of the department or even one of the school's senior managers. This is an opportunity for you to begin to sell yourself as a 'good' teacher who wants to be promoted and both wants and needs to take on more responsibility. It should then move towards deciding your professional development needs and, perhaps more importantly, to set your future targets. This is where you can suggest things like, 'In 6 months' time I want to be head of year' or, 'By this time next year I want to be deputy head/leader of geography etc'. You are telling an influential colleague what it is that you want and where you want to move to in the future. At the same time you need to be able to suggest that you are already widening your role in school and moving beyond the classroom. If you complete **Activity 7.2** (p. 149) before you have your performance management meeting you will be in a better position to argue that you are ready for greater responsibility because you will be able to list all the contributions to the school or the department that you have made already.

Working with colleagues and resolving conflict

Many of the points made in this section can be linked to the 'I'm OK, you're OK school' (Chapter 1, p. 9) How you and your colleagues relate to each other is extremely important, especially if you want to work well as part of a team or even lead a subject or department. To do this well, it is useful to understand as much as possible about how relationships might work.

At a basic level you will have easily recognisable **positive** and **negative** colleagues. The positive colleagues will be cooperative, responsive and easy to work with. On the other hand, the negative colleagues are likely to be poor team members, indifferent and wanting their own way. Within any school or department there are bound to be teachers like this, who have problems sustaining the effort of discussing important issues, and who find the whole business of moving forward and raising standards difficult and threatening. One person's negative reactions can, unfortunately, have quite a devastating effect on decisions, forward planning and change. They can drag down any feelings of happiness and excitement and can undermine all your successes and hard work. It is always difficult to suggest how to deal with colleagues like this without marginalising them and making them even more negative and disillusioned.

One way forward is to understand that they are often nervous of change or feel threatened by it. They frequently seem able to shut out their awareness of any problems and by trying to avoid important issues can build up a whole list of distracting points (that are usually relatively meaningless) for any task in hand. What they seem to have in common is a list of blocking phrases that will take a team leader or even a positive colleague all their powers of assertion and persuasion to neutralise. But, they cannot be allowed to succeed. If they do, nothing will get done and everything will stand still. This can be disastrous for the department, the subject, the school, and more importantly, the pupils. **Activity 7.3** (p. 150) lists some of the most common blocking statements. You will have heard many of them before and it will be useful to suggest how you would change them to a more positive outlook. If you do chair meetings or lead a decision-making team — or aspire to do this — then you will need to think of as many positive skills as you can.

Your colleagues will all have their own foibles, attitudes and personality types. What each department and school needs to aim for and you can play an important part in this — is a situation where in order to maintain positive relationships you will: